BEING
HUMAN

Being Human

THE ART
OF FEELING ALIVE

By Haskell E. Bernstein, M.D.

GARDNER PRESS, INC.
New York   London   Sydney

GARDNER PRESS, INC.
19 Union Square West
New York, New York 10003

All foreign orders except Canada and South America to:

Afterhurst Limited
Chancery House
319 City Road
London, N1, England

Library of Congress Cataloging-in-Publication Data

Bernstein, Haskell.
  Being human: the art of feeling alive / Haskell E. Bernstein.
  p.   cm.
  Includes bibliographical references.
  ISBN 0-89876-157-3 : $21.95.—ISBN 0-89876-175-1 (pbk.) : $14.95
  1. Happiness.   I. Title.
  BF575.H27B465   1990
  158—dc20   90-33015
                                                                  CIP

PRINTED IN THE UNITED STATES OF AMERICA

Book Design by Sidney Solomon

For Patsy

Contents

Contents

Acknowledgments

I wish to express my gratitude: to Morris Sklansky for our continuing dialogue over many years that helped me to crystallize many of my concepts; to Paul Bohannon, Francoise Meltzer, Stanley Reiter, M. Barrie Richmond, E. James Anthony, Ann and Mark Scheckner, and Stuart Brent for their encouragement and helpful suggestions upon reading the manuscript in its various stages; to Laurie Bernstein for her excellent editorial help throughout the project; to my wife and children for their love and patient support; and finally, to all the people who have taught me about people—those I've known best have taught me most.

Haskell E. Bernstein

BEING
HUMAN

Introduction:
The Reality of Happiness

Everyone wants to feel good, to be happy, but no one has discovered the precise formula for achieving that goal. Health and wealth have their proponents, fame and glory have theirs. There are hedonists and religionists and utopian political theorists, all pointing the way in different directions. Some believe it is a matter so personal and individual that there can be no single route to follow, that one man's meat is necessarily another's poison. And there are the more pessimistic who believe it to be an illusory wish, unachievable, precluded by the ineluctable circumstances of the human condition.

I take the position that happiness is an achievable goal and that people are justified in their determination to seek it. Man's prevalent discontent through recorded history seems insufficient reason for resignation to some immutable malignant fate. Certainly some people are happy—and some are happy at least some of the time—and if some, why not more? Some limitations do stem from the "human condition." We are unable to fly on our own power, unable to breathe underwater without appropriate scuba apparatus, but nothing in the "human condition" precludes happiness and contentment.

Of course it is true that people tend to look for happiness in many of the wrong places, but that is understandable since the human organism is constructed to perceive the outside world more clearly than it is able to look inside. It's rather like the man who persists in searching for his lost keys within the ring of light cast by a street lamp, convinced that he'd never be able to find them in the surrounding darkness. In time, however, he must conclude that the keys are not there within the available light, and then he must contrive ways to shed more light upon the darkness. The continued effort is even more warranted if the keys he seeks are keys to happiness.

This book attempts to deal with some of the internal issues that bear upon the quest, not as a guidebook pointing out yet another direction to follow, but as an examination of the meaning and the mechanisms of feeling good. While happiness depends largely upon the interaction of the individual and his world, feeling good about one's self is an internal matter and a precondition for achieving happiness. For far too long we have sought the route to happiness almost exclusively in the external conditions of our lives, and we have failed to pay sufficient attention to the very nature of the human being, to those factors within the individual that allow happiness to happen. I leave the arguments about which external circumstances contribute best to happiness to the sociologists, economists, theologians, and all others who believe that the answers are to be found someplace out there. I have seen too many of the rich and the powerful and the morally pure who did not feel good, did not find happiness thereby, and who have convinced me that our externalities are of only secondary importance. It is, then, a book about psychology, our least exact science, for feeling good must inevitably involve feeling, and feelings are the central domain of psychology.

FEELING GOOD AND OPTIMAL FUNCTION

Now, it is a peculiar fact of history that psychology and its therapeutic disciplines, psychiatry and psychoanalysis, have, from the start, been directed primarily toward the alleviation of pain and suffering. And that is a worthy goal but it is not enough, for man wants more than freedom from pain. Just as medicine in general has shown signs of beginning to turn from an exclusive emphasis on the treatment of illness toward the promotion of optimal physical function, so must psychology turn from its predominant focus on alleviation of pain toward further exploration of the realm of optimal psychic (mental) function.

There is a parallel ambiguity that attaches to our conventional use of the term, *normal,* as it applies to health. I recall one physician's statement that "having two or three colds a year is normal," implying that being ill can be normal. And that is correct when the term *normal* is given its statistical meaning, "average." But medicine also employs the term to mean "optimal." Given one's choice, everyone would prefer optimal health to average health. Freedom from pain is good; feeling good is better.

Our quest, then, is for the meaning of optimal psychic function. Realizing in advance that perfection is rarely, if ever, achieved, we are relieved of that excessive burden. But I believe that it's safe to say that most people feel that they might function better than they do, and there can be nothing wrong with each one striving to achieve one's own best level.

Indeed, my partial answer to the riddle is that feeling good is tied to the conviction that one is using one's self effectively and well. From that conviction, and from that alone, derives each person's self-esteem. It is quite impossible to imagine someone with low self-esteem being happy and, conversely, happy people inevitably have high self-esteem. The two go together.

The concept of self-esteem is widely known and is probably just as widely confused and misunderstood. Many believe that self-esteem derives from being esteemed by others, while some confuse esteem with love and blunder into the misconception that self-esteem and self-love (narcissism) are the same. It is imperative that we come to understand that self-esteem is a self-judgment: a judgment each person makes

4

Introduction: The Reality of Happiness

about how well he functions for himself. It is *not* a product of how well someone else thinks he functions, nor is it a product of how well he functions for another. In either of those cases he is subject to the whim of others and so must feel helpless. I maintain that helplessness is the condition of lowest self-esteem, and that therefore any attempt to gain self-esteem by submitting to the judgment of others is doomed to fail. Many spend their whole lives in a futile effort to please others and end up despising themselves.

This is not to be construed as a philosophy of arrogance, of "I'm out for myself and everyone else be damned." Inter-personal relationships are extremely important to every one of us, and insensitivity to the feelings of others can only accrue damage to ourselves. It is fundamentally human to want close and intimate relationships with others. But the most basic, most important, relationship one can have is the relationship one has with one's self. Unless one can be close, intimate, with one's self one cannot be close and intimate with another. To be intimate with one's self means only to be open and honest to one's self about one's self. If you are driven to keep secrets about yourself from yourself, then you cannot possibly be honest about yourself to another.

As helplessness is the condition of lowest self-esteem, autonomy, *self*-mastery, is the condition of highest self-esteem. Autonomy is the conviction of being truly in charge of oneself—not the hapless victim of unknowable forces, external or internal. It may seem strange to hear a purported scientist, convinced of the deterministic nature of our universe, speak of free will and choice. Yet it is not so strange, for one may know more or know less about the forces by which one is moved and one may feel that his action is or is not influenced by his own judgment. Even though his judgment, at any given moment, is strictly determined by his past, still it is *his* judgment, his own unique and individual judgment. It is this conviction that one knows by what forces he is moved and that his behavior is influenced by his judgment that creates the conviction of free will and choice—of autonomy or self-mastery.

We are, of course, moved by many external forces, but that is not the focus of our present investigation. Our concern here is with the forces within—our own feelings—for feelings are the internal forces that move us to action. We eat when we *feel* hunger, we engage in sex when we *feel* sexual desire, we explore when we *feel* curiosity. Always it is feeling that moves us to action. But we are also aware that feelings sometimes cause discomfort and pain. Anger may threaten relationships that we value and upon which we depend. Love leaves us vulnerable to the hurt of rejection and loss. Fear, anxiety, and uncertainty often make us hesitate, stumble, at precisely those moments when we should act decisively and forthrightly. Greed prompts us to act in ways that others, and that we ourselves, consider distasteful. The list can go on and on. For almost every feeling we can easily identify some real or potential disadvantage. And so there is a strong tendency to seek a comfortable security in the avoidance of feelings. When we accede to that tendency, we pay a terrible price.

IMPEDIMENTS TO HAPPINESS

I propose that the fear of our own feelings is the most direct and immediate impediment to our search for happiness. We have a number of means by which we can try to avoid our feelings, and each of those means carries its own cost.

First, we may directly avoid all situations that are likely to evoke feelings, but that leads to a life of constriction and barren isolation.

Second, we may avoid conscious awareness of our feelings by repression. While the mechanism of repression will be discussed in detail later, for now it need only be explained that repression of feelings is not eradication of feelings—the feelings persist but are kept out of conscious awareness. If the repression barriers are weak and the repressed feelings threaten to break into conscious awareness, anxiety is the price we pay. But if the repression barriers are strong and repression of feelings is extensive and successful, then the stage is set for that widespread malaise that I have identified as "chronic boredom," characterized by alienation, apathy, and restless dissatisfaction.

The conventional view holds boredom to be a trivial emotion, but I maintain that chronic boredom is a real and serious malaise that causes widespread suffering, often leading to severe depression and even to suicide. The case studies in Chapter 4 attempt to demonstrate the coexistence of chronic boredom with other more widely recognized categories of emotional illness that often obscure the underlying condition of chronic boredom. It is difficult to determine whether modes of emotional illness change as times change, or increasing knowledge permits us to perceive more clearly hitherto unrecognized forms of psychopathology. In either case, there is reason to believe that chronic boredom is today the primary character neurosis, whereas hysteria and obsessive-compulsive neurosis were the prevalent forms of psychopathology in Europe during Freud's time. Perhaps repression, long recognized to be the primary defense against conscious awareness of feelings, has been strengthened over time by cultural reinforcement, so that the anxiety of a weaker repression in Freud's time has culminated in the chronic boredom of stronger and more successful repression today.

The third technique we employ for the avoidance of feelings is called transference. This is an unconscious misperception of something present as though it were something from the past. So one person unwittingly perceives his wife's headache as though it were his mother's typical hypochondriacal complaint; another misperceives her boss's strong and efficient leadership as her father's tyranny. When Freud called attention to this phenomenon, he attributed its cause to an irreducible "repetition compulsion" which he postulated to be a biological tendency in all living matter, a tendency to return to an earlier state. My view of it differs (see discussion in Chapter 5) for I see no evidence to support his thesis of a mysterious "repetition compulsion." Instead, I see transference to be a defense against novelty, enabling us to avoid those feelings which might be evoked in novel situations, feelings which we could not anticipate and for which we might not be prepared. So we distort present perception of the novel in order to see only an illusory familiar past that will evoke no unanticipated feelings.

Often it is a matter of preferring to see "the devil we know." One is puzzled to see a woman select and marry a husband who is as brutal and tyrannical as was her father, and it's easy to assume that she was so fixated upon her father that she was impelled to perpetuate the past in the present. Usually that is not the explanation. Instead, she has chosen to perpetuate a known and familiar misery rather than to take the risks of an unknown and novel experience of love. Deeper investigation reveals that her husband is not really just like her father, but close enough to enable her to maintain the misperception that he is. She deems it safer to see it that way.

Beyond the direct costs of these mechanisms for the avoidance of feelings—barren isolation caused by direct avoidance, anxiety or chronic boredom caused by repression, and chaos in interpersonal relationships and distorted perception of the world caused by transference—all three of them require some degree of loss of autonomy, lowering self-esteem, for each of those mechanisms impels behaviors over which we have little or no conscious control.

This fear of our feelings and our efforts to avoid them is further complicated by our failure to understand the very nature of feelings, despite all of the efforts of science and of philosophy to fathom the riddle of their significance. My work has led me to a concept of feelings which, while not a total explanation of the nature of feelings, emphasizes the essential role that they play in adaptation and makes explicit their valued contribution to the experience of life. It provides the basis for an alternative to Freud's rather cumbersome theory of motivation by which he attempted to explain human behavior as the result of two irreducible and often opposing drives (first, erotic and ego drives, later Eros and Thanatos). That reductionism may have satisfied Freud's wish to explain conflict in human psychic life, but it left for us the impossible task of trying to understand the rich complexity of life in terms of a simplistic dualism. For example, love then had to be understood as an expression of the erotic drive, thereby binding love and sex. When love appeared without accompanying sexuality, as in love of child or parent or friend, then new and ad hoc theories like neutralization and sublimation had to be invented to explain that appearance of love without apparent sexuality. Similarly, assertiveness was tied to the death instinct, Thanatos, the source of hostility and destructiveness, and ways had to be found to explain that away.

The alternative view that I present requires no abstraction like "drives" to explain motivation. Instead, I hold that we are moved by our many feelings, each of which reflects some disequilibrium in one of our many interacting systems, and each of which is to be accorded its independent existence and individual attention. No ad hoc theories need be created to disentangle them from each other. Beyond that, it is the impelling quality of feelings, pressing always toward discharge in action, that we experience as energy, vitality, zest. And when we are cut off from our feelings we are apathetic and the world seems dreary and dull.

Make no mistake; we cannot be rid of our feelings, for they are intrinsic to our being. We may seek to avoid them by the mechanisms described above, but when and as we succeed in that effort, we have amputated a central and intrinsic part of ourselves. Those who ask "the meaning of life" are only seeking a compensatory intellectualized explanation to replace the lost significance that feelings give to life. Those who are feelingful participants in life have no such need to ask its meaning.

Here is our dilemma, then: feelings, intrinsic to our being, are what make our lives significant to us, and yet those same feelings are sometimes the source of our pain and discomfort. Does this preclude the possibility of happiness? Only if we insist that the happy person *never* experience pain and discomfort, and that would be most unrealistic. Negative things do happen. Loved ones do die or leave us. Conflict and tensions do arise. We cannot eradicate all suffering, but we can attempt to lessen it and to use ourselves to best advantage. That would be happiness enough.

Some believe that civilization is the culprit, placing restraints upon our feelings and thereby depriving us of the happiness we might feel if we were free. Freud's *Civilization and Its Discontents* (1930) expresses such a view and is often described as pessimistic, for its explicit message declares that we do pay a price for civilization, the curtailment of instinctual gratification. He states, "the feeling of happiness produced by indulgence of a wild, untamed craving is incomparably more intense than is the satisfying of a curbed desire."

Were we to accept that view, our prospects would be gloomy, at best. Man would be in the position of having to choose between civilization and happiness and that would be no choice at all, for certainly there would be little hope for happiness without civilization, without a social structure. Must civilized man forego happiness? There is room to question Freud's position on this matter. For one thing, he never did pursue the concept of happiness very far, and his statements in *Civilization and Its Discontents* would seem to equate happiness with intensity of sensual pleasure. Most people mean much more than that when they speak of happiness, yet it is true that we have no precise description or definition of what we mean by that term. We know it when we feel it, yet when poets, philosophers, and psychologists confront the concept they nearly always conclude that happiness is so individualistic, so variable, and so subjective that it cannot be defined in any consistent way.

Introduction: The Reality of Happiness
TOWARD A DEEPER UNDERSTANDING

There is another possibility. We may not yet know enough about man's psychology to be able to recognize all the consistent elements that contribute to the feeling of happiness. With a better understanding of what constitutes the feeling of happiness we may discover that happiness is quite compatible with civilization or we may find that civilization, itself, is not the obstruction, but that certain modifiable aspects of civilization as we know it interfere with the realization of man's goal.

For example, is it true that "curbed desires" are the inevitable consequence of being civilized? In Freud's statement about "wild, untamed craving" and "curbed desire" cited above, that seems to be the clear implication. And yet the purpose of civilization is *not* to lessen the intensity of human feelings but to put curbs upon man's behavior. It is the proper business of society to regulate the interactions between people—to regulate how man behaves with his fellow man. But behavior is not feeling. Feelings are the personal possession of every one of us—they belong to each of us alone—and society has no right to tamper with them, to try to change or diminish their intensities.

Feelings do motivate behavior, and intense feelings do impel more strongly to action. Then *one* way to control man's behavior is by diminishing his motivation to act, by curbing the intensity of his feelings. Perhaps that is what the religionists in early time recognized either consciously or unconsciously when they took the step to proclaim that not only was it a crime to act against one's fellow man, but also a sin to *feel* like doing so.

The proper business of civilization is not the curbing of man's feelings but the informing of his judgment. To take away or diminish his feelings is to deprive him of his essential humanity. Man, free to experience the full range and intensity of his feelings, can use the full power of his informed judgment to determine how he shall act upon those feelings. This is the crucial distinction, often lost, between the experience of feelings and the expression of feelings.

Lurking behind these efforts to control man's behavior, either by curtailing his feelings or by other means, lies the conviction that man is wild and evil, and therefore must be tamed and trained to be good. When we view the present scene and when we look back upon history, there is enough evidence to convince us of man's persistent inhumanity to man. What we do not know, and cannot yet judge, is whether or not such behavior is inevitable. It is possible that we ourselves, misled by conventional expectations, create the conditions in life that foster brutishness. Perhaps it is the continued effort to tame and to train the human being that, itself, creates the frustration, anger, and greed that have marked history. Altering our long-held conventional view of mankind could remove the need to force the human animal to conform to some preconceived notion of what we think the human being should be but is not.

It is my view that man is fundamentally a loving creature who, throughout history, has been consistently taught to be afraid to love. That, in itself, would cause sufficient frustration to account for much of his anger, his rage, through time. As I shall attempt to demonstrate, there is reason to believe that love is the central and most pervasive of all of man's feelings. Unfortunately, our failure to have recognized and understood this has led us to try to tame people and to train them to be loving as they grow, and what we have accomplished thereby is mainly a fear of loving. We have much to learn about human feelings in general, but most importantly we must eventually come to understand what love is and why it is so centrally important in human life.

Our deepest penetration into the understanding of the mind came with Freud's creative work centered upon the neuroses, those dramatic and seeming bizarre disturbances of mental function. It is quite reasonable that this became his starting point, for the smoothly functioning human organism affords little opportunity to view the particular interacting mechanisms of his vastly complex system. Freud focused upon the dysjunctions inherent in the neuroses and thereby got his foot in the door and forced it open wider. But Freud's goal was not the narrow one of understanding the psychopathology of the neuroses. That was important, but it was only a part of his much wider aspiration to achieve the formulation of a general psychology, a broad understanding of how and why man behaves.

The history of the development of psychoanalytic psychology since its beginning with Freud is a fascinating story of momentous discoveries, but it is rather off the point of this work. I wish to refer to that history only fleetingly, in an effort to fill in, with broad strokes, how we came to be where we are.

The early discoveries were exciting and attracted a circle of adventurous colleagues who worked with Freud to push those discoveries further toward a complete understanding of man's psychology. A particularly significant step in that direction came as Freud (1908, 1916), Karl Abraham (1921, 1924), and Wilhelm Reich (1928, 1929, 1930) contributed to the formulation of characterology and character neuroses. Now they were dealing not with the relatively simple localizable symptom neurosis and its isolatable causes but were using the knowledge gained about human development to understand how heredity and experience interacted to organize the individual's character—that is, the individual's typical and habitual attitudes and modes of behavior. Character came to be recognized as a specific and individualized organization for the purpose of adaptation and Reich (1930) brilliantly suggested that the symptom neurosis arose as a localized emergency mechanism to fill a breach in the adaptive efficacy of the character organization. Since that time the therapeutic focus of psychoanalysis has swung from symptom analysis to character analysis.

Now the process of exploration became harder. The openings provided by the symptom neuroses had led to the deeper and broader understanding of man in terms of the development of his character, but there the openings became less obvious. It was one thing to investigate a symptom neurosis wherein, for example, an individual had a hand-washing compulsion, a specific and obvious behavior that appeared to be meaningless and nonadaptive to that individual as well as to everyone else. The patient saw the behavior as an undesirable intrusion upon himself, a kind of foreign object in his psychic life that he wished to be expunged. It was quite another matter to investigate the workings of a compulsive character structure with its behavioral manifestations of punctiliousness, excessive neatness, and thrift, for these behaviors did not seem strange or foreign to the individual who was so constituted. He did not want to be rid of such behavior—indeed, he often defended it strenuously as being socially constructive and valuable, the right way to be. That he suffered in his capacity to work, to love, to play, was a matter of concern to him that he wished to have corrected, but it was not an easy matter for him to see the connections between those things and his compulsive insistence on promptness and cleanliness.

In the character disorders we were dealing with expressions of psychopathology that were far more prevalent and much more subtle; subtle because they were common and because they could be justified on grounds of having social value. Still, psychoanalytic technique evolved to cope with these resistances to exploration and the examination of character structure and its formation proceeded.

We have, thereby, come a long way in understanding human psychology in its broadest sense, yet discomfort, discontent, and dissatisfaction remain widespread. Psychoanalytic psychology is frequently called into question and judged to have failed, by some within the profession as well as by many outside. New therapies spring up all around us, some returning to the mystical and magical, some simply opportunistic, as well as some that are serious though often misguided attempts to find a better way.

I am clearly committed to psychoanalytic psychology,

simply on the grounds that a body of knowledge that has come to explain so much about human behavior cannot be condemned and dismissed just because it has not yet been able to explain and correct everything in man's psychic life. Perhaps it will never explain everything, but if that were the criterion for acceptance for any body of knowledge then physics, too, would be unacceptable, being as yet unable to finally explain such basic natural phenomena as gravity, light, matter, energy, and so on.

Psychoanalytic psychology remains incomplete in two major ways. First, there is much more to be learned and the going gets harder the deeper we penetrate the workings of the mind. The step from symptom neuroses to character neuroses took us from the study of dramatic and often bizarre isolated behaviors to the investigation of broader, more subtle, and therefore more difficult, aspects of general psychology. Now, I believe, it is time to take another similar step to try to discover the reasons for, the sources of, man's prevalent discontent and the elusiveness of his goal of happiness. The difficulty of the prospect before us can only be appreciated as we realize that this investigation leads us into an area of experience that is so widespread that a large segment of humanity through the ages has considered it to reflect not a problem of man, but the condition of man. The view that I shall here present is that the prevalence of human discontent is not inevitable, but stems in large part from our inadequate understanding of what feelings are and the fear of directly dealing with them.

The second major way in which psychoanalytic psychology is incomplete relates to the internal inconsistencies and errors that exist within the present framework of psychoanalytic theory. One must understand that this relatively young science has had a dynamic and prodigious growth in its short span. Theories formulated to embrace new discoveries had often to be altered, sometimes abandoned and replaced, to accommodate even newer discoveries, and all of this at a very rapid rate. Contradictions and inconsistencies became embedded in the rapidly evolving theoretical structure, and these require careful reassessment and realignment to strengthen its fabric without destroying its value. As in all fields of science, the two processes become intertwined; new findings and reformulations of existing theories proceed in step.

It is my impression that the study of characterology remains incomplete. The currently accepted view of character and its formation places emphasis on its adaptive function. Character is a good and necessary human attribute in that it enables us to cope, to live in our world and in a society. There can be little argument with that position, yet there has been little attention paid to the other side of the matter, the question of what is the individual cost of having a character structure that is largely determined by society's conventional and limited view of man. It is possible that we ourselves unwittingly twist and distort each person's developing character in accordance with societal assumptions and expectations, forcing the individual to conform to molds structured by civilization's inherited false premises. And then we deem those character structures "normal" when, within our society, they fit an average expectancy.

The human being is not static. Like all biological organisms, man's structure is modified by the conditions in which he lives.

It is time to begin to trust the human to be human, but that will be no easy task. Through the ages our culture has developed and maintained what I hold to be an erroneous view of mankind; a view that perceives man to be an inherently evil creature that must be trained to become a good human. It is difficult to change those deeply ingrained cultural attitudes but it is not an impossible feat; we may yet be able to learn that man is a loving creature from the start.

Then, in the light of a brighter expectation, his character structure will grow to a more humane configuration, one more consonant with the goal of happiness. The more we understand about the complex mechanism that is man, the more we will be able to contribute to that felicitous change.

Feelings are a fundamental aspect of our being. To use ourselves effectively and well we must overcome our fear of feelings and be free to take the risk of being the loving creatures that we are.

If we can do this, will we then be happy? Happiness requires the participation of a benevolent and provident world, and our reality is not always so disposed. But within those limits, he who uses himself effectively and well is in the best position to allow happiness to happen.

1

Self-Esteem

" I think I have an inferiority complex," John C. told me in his first consultation.

You will come to know a great deal more about John C. later, in Chapter 4, but for now permit me to introduce him as an attractive young man of twenty-one who had dropped out of college a year before and who continued to feel quite miserable.

I asked him what he meant by "inferiority complex," how it manifested itself. He explained that he always felt that he was not good enough—not smart enough, not athletic enough, not sufficiently informed to be an interesting conversationalist. There were any number of things in which he felt he did not hit the mark. Oh, yes! He also thought that he was lazy and that he lacked sufficient courage and determination.

I showed mild surprise at his extensive list of experienced deficiencies, and of course it had little effect that I repeated some of the positive information about himself that he had supplied earlier in the session. He had graduated from a very good suburban high school in the upper ten percent of his class and had been accepted by a prestigious Eastern university—that sounded smart enough to me. And he had been on the varsity track team in high school. For over a year, since he dropped out of college, he had made it on his own, traveling around the country, supporting himself by working in short-order restaurants, on loading docks, and in a newspaper office. That seemed to me to indicate neither laziness nor a lack of courage and determination. He'd always had friends, both male and female, and had had a couple of love affairs. That suggested to me that others found him to be interesting. He nodded and said he knew all that. He didn't mean that he thought he was dumb—just not smart enough. Sure he had some courage—just not enough. Always it was "just not enough." I wondered what he thought would be enough. He shrugged and said, "More than I have, more than I am."

The picture presented by John C. is far from novel or unique. We all know people who seem to judge themselves too harshly, and many of them find some comfort in accepting the label "inferiority complex." Presumably that label has become popularly accepted because it seems to imply "I feel that I'm inferior but I'm really not—it's just that there's something wrong that makes me *think* that I'm inferior."

I want to make it very clear that I do not hold with the concept of an inferiority complex. There is no such thing. The one critical judgment that everyone makes with remarkably consistent accuracy is the evaluation of his own worth. Despite the prevalent human tendency to misperceive, to distort, to misjudge all manner of things, this one thing tends to be seen quite clearly. And that is reasonable, for each person is in the best position—perhaps the only position—to judge his own worth. He who deems himself inferior is making an accurate assessment. He *is* inferior, but in a very specific way.

SELF-ESTEEM AND OTHERS' ESTEEM

In view of the prevalence of low self-esteem, it may seem harsh to conclude that all of those people are quite accurate. That would indicate that there are a great many who are not v orth very much. The key question is, "not worth very much to whom?" As soon as the subject of a person's worth arises there is a tendency to assume that some societal judgment is involved. That is not so in this case. One can cite many examples of the "good" person who holds himself in low esteem and who persists in that view despite our repeated assurance that he is kind and considerate and contributes more than most to his society. We see him as a valuable person, but we are estimating different things. We are judging his worth to society while he is describing his worth to himself, and the latter is the real meaning of self-esteem. He will be grateful for the expression of our esteem, he may even feel much better because of it, for a while, but it will not alter his self-evaluation one iota. As Alexander Pope put it long ago, in "An Essay on Man" (1733–34):

> One self-approving hour whole years outweighs
> of stupid starers and of loud huzzas.
> And more true joy Marcellus exil'd feels
> than Caesar with a senate at his heels.

Accurate as people are in estimating their worth to themselves, it is extremely rare to find one who consciously knows how and why he really arrived at that estimation. There is a great deal of confusion surrounding the concept of self-esteem; very little understanding of its meaning and its mechanism. The fundamental error stems from the failure to understand that self-esteem is a *self*-judgment—a judgment made about one's self by one's self. Given that failure of understanding, it is easy to compound the confusion. Self-esteem becomes confused with esteem from others and leads many to conclude that self-esteem is simply the product of esteem from others. Then they spend themselves in the futile effort to win as much esteem from as many others as they can, hoping thereby to bolster their own low self-esteem. Then, like John C., they try to understand their low self-esteem in terms of their imagined failure to win sufficient esteem from others.

They try to explain their failure in terms that fit some

moral, societal, or interpersonal code or system of measurement. One person thinks that his low opinion of himself is the result of having undesirable or evil thoughts, feelings, and impulses, even though he is intellectually aware that these are shared by multitudes. Another explains that he has accomplished nothing substantial, has contributed nothing of significance, so he sees himself to be unsubstantial, insignificant. No matter that he agrees with your argument that he has achieved and contributed at least as much as have those around him, still his opinion remains fixed. A third finds his explanation in his lack of sufficient intelligence to be attractive to others—or he is physically unattractive, or clumsy, or unable to dance well, lacks social attributes—the list of rationalizations is varied and extensive. But they are rationalizations, all, and none of them are the real and accurate basis for low self-esteem.

One cannot dismiss those rationalizations as unimportant just because they are inaccurate, however, for they profoundly influence the course of many peoples' lives. The person who decides that he has little worth because he is poor (an easy and common mistranslation in our culture) determines to correct his situation by dedicating his life to the pursuit of profit. Sacrificing many other aspects of life, he finally makes his first million only to find his self-esteem unchanged by it. He often decides that this is due to his new vantage point as millionaire which more clearly reveals how many others are multimillionaires, and the pursuit continues, but always with the same result. No amount of wealth is sufficient to the task.

Another familiar pattern may be found in the perpetual student. Believing his low opinion of himself to be based upon his inadequate intellect, he determines to achieve a college degree. Then, he thinks, he will have demonstrated his worth. Finally granted his B.A. or B.S., he finds himself unchanged. The college degree does not enhance his self-esteem. Instead, the formerly prized degree is diminished by his own low self-esteem. He believes that if he could get it, it can't really be worth very much. So he sets out for a master's degree, and next a Ph.D., and then a law degree—and so on. He may spend his whole life climbing that same wrong hill, vaguely aware that it is not accomplishing the purpose, and being driven ever harder in the same direction by that vague awareness. It is not unlike the high school boy who believes that his self-esteem will be greatly augmented by winning the prettiest, most popular girl in the class. He pursues her and wins her—and then soon loses interest in her because if she can be interested in him then she must not be worth much herself. Their dilemma might seem almost humorous were the common consequences less tragic.

ESTEEM AND LOVE

Another very significant source of confusion about the meaning of self-esteem stems from the failure to adequately distinguish between esteem and love. Self-esteem and self-love (narcissism) become mistakenly blurred, mixed, and interchangeable, and that confusion largely accounts for the present popular focus on narcissism. Issues of self-esteem are seen and treated as though they were problems of narcissism, and that kind of error can lead us far astray.

Poets and philosophers have recognized for a long time that love is blind, and we accept that, recognizing that love is a feeling that follows no apparent logic or reason. On the other hand, *esteem,* a word that derives from the same root as the word *estimate,* refers to a process that is open-eyed and judgmental. On that basis alone, we must conclude that loving and esteeming are two quite different processes involving very different psychological functions. Love is feeling; esteem is judgment.

We do tend to love what we esteem, just as we tend to esteem what we love. That love and esteem can affect each other is clear, but that does not make them a unity. Freud called our attention to the typical human tendency to overestimate the object of love. He pointed out that when a man falls in love with a woman he thinks that she is the most beautiful, the most perfect woman in all the world. And fond parents "are impelled to ascribe to the child all manner of perfections which sober observation would not confirm . . ." (Freud, 1914, p. 91). But this common concurrence of love and esteem (or overestimation) should not lead us to the erroneous conclusion that they are the same. Indeed, literature and life are replete with tragic tales of those who loved intensely someone they did not esteem.

THE "DOUBLE" SELF-EVALUATION

The truly narcissistic person does pose an apparent problem for our discussion of self-esteem. Since we know that there is a strong tendency to overestimate the object of love, we should not be surprised that he who loves himself intensely would also tend to *over*estimate himself. And, indeed, it is typical of the truly narcissistic that they hold very grandiose estimations of themselves. How does one square that with the earlier assertion that one's self-esteem is always accurate? Certainly, a grandiose overestimation of self cannot be an accurate estimation of self. The key to this riddle lies in the fragility of the narcissistic person's grandiose self-esteem. The very slightest insult or slight tends to puncture his grandiosity like a pinprick to a balloon, and we find that just behind that grandiosity is an ever-lurking sense of abject worthlessness. There are two self-estimations, a grandiose one covering over an extremely low self-esteem. As object of his own love, his self is overesteemed. However, as subject, he is aware of how poorly he functions and that determines his low self-esteem.

It is the person's fundamental subjective experience of his own function that determines his accurate self-esteem.

There is another group of people, far more numerous than the narcissistic, who also seem to have a double self-estimation that resembles the situation of the narcissist. Because of the superficial similarity this much larger group of people are often mistakenly confused with the narcissistic, but they are not truly so—they do not really love themselves excessively. On the contrary, they are very much aware of their own low self-esteem and seek to hide that low self-esteem from others by erecting a facade of haughty superiority and arrogance. This defensive facade of superiority is not an overestimation born of love but derives from the common mistaken notion that "how others see me will determine how I will see myself—if I can make others esteem me I will esteem myself." For these people the high and the low self-esteem exist side by side in conscious awareness. Perhaps they are best characterized by a remark attributed to Groucho Marx. When asked if he belonged to a certain exclusive country club he replied, "I would never join a club that was willing to accept me as a member."

THE BASIS OF SELF-ESTEEM

Are there any who have a genuine high self-esteem? Of course! Some fortunate people do have a truly high regard for themselves and they easily can be distinguished from the narcissistic and from the defensively superior by their friendliness and openness, their comfort with themselves and with others. They tend to attract people to them without having to make an effort to do so, for we all admire those who think well of themselves. External circumstances permitting, they tend to be happy people.

Self-Esteem

The desire for self-approval, for high self-esteem, is strong in all of us. Mark Twain suggested that the hunger for self-approval may be called the "Master Passion" (1906), and everyone is aware, within himself, of how strong a wish it is. At the same time, few would deny the pleasurable effect of having the esteem of others. Those with high self-esteem still enjoy and want esteem from others—but they don't feel that they *need* it. Low self-esteem becomes a powerful incentive to seek the esteem of others as a compensation, especially when that individual has little inkling of what self-esteem really is and from what it really derives. Then he will bend his efforts to winning the approval of all around him and will even often misidentify his wish to be esteemed as a longing to be loved. This creates the not uncommon picture of the egocentric person with what appears to be an insatiable wish to be loved and, again, such people are often mistakenly described as narcissistic. They are not narcissistic, they do not love themselves excessively, but they do suffer from a low self-esteem and from the common confusion of self-esteem with esteem from others, and the common confusion of esteem with love. They must learn that self-esteem is the judgment each person makes about how well he functions for himself.

But what does it mean to "function well for one's self"? Perhaps an analogy can clarify the issue. You have an automobile that runs well. It starts when you want it to start; its brakes are good and it stops when you wish it. It steers easily, it goes where you want it to go, in all kinds of weather, and its gas mileage is high, so it gets you to your destination economically. I need not tell you that anyone who possesses a car of that description esteems it highly. On the other hand, if your automobile is difficult to start, undependable in its performance, has brakes that sometimes fail, and guzzles gasoline in excessive quantities, you will probably hold it in low esteem. If yours is the second car, no amount of praise of it by others will change your judgment. No matter that they love its beauty, admire its power, respect its price, you know how it performs, and you will not esteem it well.

And so it is with each person's own self-organization. As he knows that he starts easily, stops at will, can depend upon himself in all kinds of situations, and that he can get where he is going with an economy of effort, so he will have high self-esteem. But as he knows that he cannot function well for himself, cannot depend upon his own performance, and that his performance requires excessive effort, then he will hold himself in low esteem. Of course man is a far more complex mechanism than an automobile, but the analogy is valid within the limits of the analogy.

By "self-organization" I mean the unique and characteristic integration of all that constitutes an individual: his body and his mind, his physiology and his feelings, his intellect, attitudes, experience, impulses, and defenses. What we call his character is the expression of that self-organization, manifested in typical and habitual attitudes and modes of action and reaction. And the term *self* refers to a concept each holds of his own functioning totality, a concept that he forms of his own self-organization. In other words, the self-organization is a functional agency, character is its expression, and self is its conceptualization.

What are the qualities of a self-organization, conceptualized as self, that determine that individual's high or low esteem? We have already said that each person's self-esteem reflects his judgment of the effectiveness of his own self-organization, but that is too general a statement for our purpose. What comprises effective function? We can begin by assuming that it will be described differently by each person: the professional athlete would place primary emphasis upon physical prowess; the philosopher upon intellect; the artist, upon imagination and creativity. But no sooner will we find a successful and proficient athlete who truly values himself than we will find another equally successful and proficient, with low self-esteem. And the impression of experience is strong that intelligent philosophers and creative artists tend more to low self-esteem than to high, despite success in their chosen fields of endeavor.

The individual does not evaluate himself simply on the basis of any one function, nor even upon those multiple functions that may be involved in any one given activity. The individual is always multifaceted; the artist is not only artist, but spouse or lover as well, and perhaps breadwinner and parent or child to someone. He is also social, political; he has thoughts and he has feelings. His self-esteem will express his evaluation of his total function, not of any single part.

Of course his effective function in any one activity seems bound to contribute something positive to his overall self-evaluation, but even in this assumption we must be careful to distinguish between successful achievement of a goal and effective function in that achievement. For example, the runner may win a race, and that achievement will be pleasurable. But if he knows within himself that he did not run a good race, that he was too tight, that his timing was poor, then the pleasure of his victory will be blunted sharply by that self-knowledge. On the other hand, the runner who loses will be disappointed, but if he knows that he ran well he will think well of himself, despite the loss. And that is the meaning of the old cliché, "It's not winning or losing that counts, but how you play the game." That there are many among the great and powerful who do not value themselves highly should not be a matter for perplexity, for even great achievements, when poorly achieved, contribute little to self-esteem.

SELF-MASTERY

What we are dealing with is the issue of mastery—not in the usual sense of mastery of others or of the external world, but mastery of one's self. That is the critical issue upon which assessments of self-worth are based. And anything that interferes with that mastery of one's self diminishes self-esteem. It makes some difference if that interference comes from outside or from within, but in the long run any interference with self-mastery lowers self-esteem. The slave will be abject, whether he be slave to another or slave to some unknown and unmanageable force within himself. To be helpless is the condition of lowest self-esteem.

John C. stands as an example of the many who manage their internal affairs even less well than they are able to manage their external tasks. Fearing the consequences of their actions, they become inhibited and they block their feelings from conscious awareness. This causes their accomplishment of external tasks to be inefficient, wasteful, for then they must expend energy not only on the task, but also to overcome their own internal resistance. Because their feelings are blocked from conscious awareness to greater or lesser degree, they operate with only a fraction of the vitality, the zest, that conscious awareness of feelings brings to life. Unable to clearly see and understand their internal resistances, they focus attention upon all manner of external tasks, forcing themselves to try to accomplish ever more against their own invisible internal obstacles. But that way leads eventually to exhaustion. They feel helpless as they are pushed and pulled by unknown internal forces. They sense that their lives are not what they could and should be, and so they devalue themselves without recognizing that the problem is a lack of self-mastery.

Are we ever truly masters of ourselves? The poets tell us that we are insignificant in the face of infinity, that we are small and helpless creatures subject to the whim of unknown and unknowable forces. Perhaps, but then they are simply stating that we are not masters of our universe and that is quite beside the point. As soon as the child can crawl, can grasp the object of desire, can stand and walk, can communicate, he is, to that degree, acquiring mastery over himself. And with continuing growth and development his mastery of himself progresses. That total and absolute mastery of one's self may not be possible has little significance. What is important is that one may have a certain degree of mastery of one's self, and one's self-esteem rises or falls with that degree of mastery.

Those who are able to acknowledge and accept the full range of their feelings and who have confidence in their ability to express those feelings in appropriate and advantageous ways, are masters of their own internal realm. Mastery of this internal realm of feelings is the fundamental basis of high self-esteem.

But such mastery of one's feelings does not come easily. It requires long and deep familiarity with those feelings and with one's responses to them. Then one's feelings are like friends, dependable and safe. Their entrance does not surprise, does not threaten. Those who achieve this felicitous state are comfortable with themselves and, therefore, are comfortable with others. They can be vibrant with intensity of feeling, yet they are not "tense" in the way that the timid are, the timid and insecure who maintain a constant vigilance lest they be blind-sided by one or another of their own—but unfamiliar—feelings.

Empathy, the ability to know and to appreciate what another is feeling, hinges upon this capacity to know one's own feelings quite thoroughly. And intimacy with another is quite impossible without this intimacy with one's self.

In his search for happiness, man confronts oppressing forces and circumstances on all sides, and struggles against the helplessness that they threaten to impose. Arrayed against the natural forces of the universe are the physicists, chemists, and technologists; against physical illness, the physicians and surgeons; against social oppression, the political philosophers, statesmen, sociologists, and economists. And the battle against man's "own worst enemy" falls mainly to the psychologists, for man is often made helpless by his ignorance of, or inability to adequately manage, his own feelings. This last realm, the internal one, is the one that we are constructed to see least clearly, yet it poses the most immediate and most pervasive interference with the pursuit of our goal. Increasing mastery of the universe may assure man's survival, but his happiness will hinge upon his greater mastery of himself.

2
Feelings and Tension

Feeling good is, first of all, a feeling. This seemingly simple statement leads directly to the heart of a problem, the nature of feelings. We understand very little about what feelings are and how they arise. Although we live with our feelings all of the time we are forced to admit that the realm of feelings has so far resisted scientific efforts of understanding. There is no unified and consistent theory of feelings or affects,* despite all of the efforts of psychology, ethology, physiology, and philosophy. If we are to reach a better understanding of the meaning and mechanisms of feeling good, we first must be prepared to explore the nature of feeling, itself.

FEELINGS VERSUS SENSATIONS

We often do not know precisely what we mean when we refer to feelings. We say, "I feel angry," "I feel cold," ambiguously employing the term *feel* to refer at one time to an emotion, at another time to a sensation. This broad usage of the term embraces the totality of subjective experience, what

---

*Henceforth, the terms *feelings, affects,* and *emotions* shall be used interchangeably.

is often called "privileged communication," privileged because one's feelings and sensations can be directly known only by oneself. Yet there is a difference between sensation and feeling; we know that intuitively and we give them different names. How, then, are we to distinguish them from each other? It is not enough to base that distinction upon the location of the cause, to say that sensation comes from outside and that feelings come from within. We all experience a multitude of bodily sensations, subjective experiences of body parts and functions that arise wholly within the body and that do not, thereby, become classified as feelings. A muscle cramp is one such experience and it is immediately recognized as a sensation, even though it arises wholly within the body and has no identifiable external cause.

Often the distinction between sensation and feeling is clear and immediate: love is a feeling, touch is a sensation. But what then of hunger? In the not very distant past hunger was considered to be a sensation caused by the contractions of an empty stomach, but more recent advances in surgical technique have quashed that easy answer. There are many people now who have had their stomachs totally removed for the treatment of peptic ulcer or other disorders, and those people continue to experience hunger quite without benefit of contracting stomachs. Hunger is a subjective experience that defies attempts at localization. We know it when we feel it. We do not doubt its reality, yet we cannot point to a particular place and say, with conviction, that that is where we feel hunger.

I propose that this is the single consistent feature that distinguishes feeling from sensation: We cannot localize feelings but always have a conviction about the locality of a sensation. We see with our eyes, hear with our ears, and when we experience the sensation of touch we can point to a definite area of our skin that has made contact with an object. We cannot know in the same way just where it is that we feel love or anger, shame or guilt.

Sensations Accompany Feelings

The importance of a precise distinction between feeling and sensation is not to be underestimated, for our past failure to make that distinction clear has contributed in large measure to our confusion about feelings. It is a peculiar attribute of feelings that they are often—perhaps always—attended by specific accompanying sensations. While the feelings are not localizable, their accompanying sensations are, and that has created ambiguity for poets and scientists alike. Poets tell us that love is felt in the heart, anger and fear in the gut. But that is poetic license which allows substitution of sensation for feeling. Science is allowed no such license and when it lapses into poetic simile its theories become tangled and contradictory. Clarity demands that we recognize that the person who feels hunger may often experience the accompanying sensation of stomach contractions, hunger pangs, but that those sensations do not constitute the feeling of hunger. Similarly, feeling love may be accompanied by heart or chest sensations, but those sensations do not constitute the feeling of love.

Some seem to rely heavily upon these accompanying sensations to inform themselves of their feelings. This becomes especially clear in the compulsive neurotic character with marked blocking of conscious affect who often sounds as though his only means of contact with feeling were through his awareness of sensations: "My face feels hot . . . like I'm blushing . . . so maybe I'm feeling embarrassed about something." Or, "I feel my heart pounding . . . I guess I'm feeling scared." Such reports tend always to be speculative, the sensations serving as a basis for surmise about the underlying feelings that are not directly and consciously experienced. That is not the typical and ordinary course of events. Most people experience their feelings directly and unequivocally and, although they may experience the accompanying sensations as well, they do not have to rely upon thsoe sensations to know their feelings.

Feelings and Tension

Because we know where we experience sansation, and because we can usually point to the immediate or proximal cause of the sensory event, we find it easy to regard sensation as part of the natural world. Feelings, on the other hand, seem mysterious. We do not know where we feel them and often we are unable to specify their immediate causes, so we tend to attribute their existence to mystical forces, demonic or divine. Intellectually, we know better. Feelings, too, must be part of the natural world and there must be a natural explanation for them.

Freud did not achieve a complete theory of feelings, but he did make a number of assertions about feelings that have strongly influenced the direction of thought about them. Some of those assertions, unfortunately, appear to be contradictory, compounding the confusion. On one hand, he described feelings as the psychic representation of physiologically based "drives" (1915b) a view that holds that feelings originate in bodily processes and secondarily become manifest in the mind. On the other hand, he also claimed that feelings were discharge processes, stating that "affectivity manifests itself essentially in motor (secretory and vasomotor) discharge resulting in an (internal) alteration of the subject's own body . . ." (1915a). The latter position suggests that feelings originate in the mind and secondarily become manifest in the body. The two stated positions are clearly in opposition to each other, for the first describes a process that moves from body to mind while the second describes movement from mind to body. It cannot be both ways. I assume that this problem arose because Freud himself failed at times to clearly distinguish feelings from their accompanying sensations. He called those accompanying sensations "affect equivalents" and that was, perhaps, a poor choice of terms for they are not truly equivalent to affects or feelings, but are simply accompaniments of feelings.

Freud conceptualized the mind according to the model of the reflex arc with its centripetal and centrifugal arms. Excitation flowing centripetally, toward the mind, was to be considered a stimulus to the mind, raising its level of excitation: excitation flowing from the mind to bodily innervations was to be considered psychic discharge, lowering the level of excitation in the mind. I hold that feelings are not themselves discharge processes but that they do *create* discharge processes that are responsible for the sensations that accompany feelings. Feelings are always a matter of stimulation of the mind, not of psychic discharge, and the secretory and vasomotor bodily changes to which Freud referred are the consequence of psychic discharge *caused* by feelings, and are experienced not as feelings but as sensations that accompany feelings.

FEELINGS AND ADAPTATION

Although we do not know at this time the explicit mechanisms responsible for feelings, I suggest that there is a way to understand a good deal about feelings, about why they exist and why they are fundamentally important in our lives. That way lies within the broad context of the concept of adaptation, for feelings can be viewed as part of a highly evolved mechanism of adaptation in man that has its antecedents throughout the whole range of living things.

In the simplest living organisms to the most complex, the intricate and sensitive mechanisms of adaptation that enable life to continue are awesome. The single-celled amoeba flows through its watery medium, moving toward and engulfing those substances that are necessary for its nutrition, and moving away from those substances that are noxious. It almost appears to know what it wants and what it should avoid, quite without benefit of brain or mind. Nor do we have to attribute this exquisitely adaptive behavior to some mysterious mental function where there is no evidence of its existence. The behavior is the strictly determined result of the physical-chemical interaction between the substance of the amoeba and the substances of its surrounding medium.

Similarly, plants tend always to grow to a configuration that provides optimal sunlight for each plant within the limits available to it, and the roots will grow long or short, shallow or deep, to provide an optimal water supply. Again, we need not attribute feelings or volition to plants to explain this behavior, for it, too, is the fixed and determined result of the physical-chemical interaction between the organism and factors in its immediate environment. For example, plants have a more rapid linear growth in shade than in sunlight, so the shaded side of the stem grows faster than the sunlit side and the stem therefore bends unerringly toward the sun. These simple and direct adaptive mechanisms in plants and in simple animals are called tropisms.

How lucky for the amoeba, for plants, that they are so cunningly contrived to assure their survival. Yet, as has been pointed out by others, it is not so mysterious. Had they not been so contrived, they would have soon ceased to exist and we might never have even known of them. Indeed, many organisms undoubtedly have evolved by chance lacking adequate adaptive mechanisms and therefore have lived but brief unnoticed moments.

As we move up the evolutionary scale to more complex organisms, we find adaptive mechanisms that are correspondingly more complex. In the insect world, tropism tends to be replaced by instinct. Now the organism's adaptive behavior is no longer determined by direct physical-chemical interaction between its own substance and that of its surrounding environment for the more complex organism carries much of its environment with it, within the structure of its own being.

The spider, for example, no longer has to exist only in a watery medium even though it needs water to survive, for it stores a supply of water within its own tissues. Even so, it is not wholly self-contained and will have to replenish its stores of water and nutriments from time to time. The web-spinning spider obtains these materials from its external environment by ingesting flies, but this process no longer resembles the direct physical-chemical attraction between the amoeba and its nutriment. The spider does not respond directly to the fly and, in fact, often will not accept a fly offered to it, seeming then not to recognize the fly as its favored source of nutriment. The spider responds, instead, to the state of balance of its own internal environment, spinning its web in response to its own nutritional demands. Only as the fly impacts the web does the spider recognize his meal. The web-spinning behavior is a fixed and rigidly determined response, not to some physical-chemical interaction between the spider and the fly, but to the particular physical-chemical state of balance in the spider's own internal environment.

In both tropism and instinct we see reflected a universal tendency in living matter to maintain a dynamic equilibrium of complex interacting physical-chemical systems. In the tropism of primitive life forms the primary focus of that equilibrium lies in the field of interaction between the organism and its immediate surrounding environment. Physical-chemical factors in the organism reacting with those factors in its environment rigidly determine the behavior of the organism at each given moment. When we come to the instinctual behavior of more complex organisms the primary focus of that dynamic equilibrium shifts to the field of the organism's internal environment. Now the tendency to maintain an equilibrium of internal interacting physical-chemical systems primarily determines behavior. That behavior is contrived to extract from the external environment those factors and substances that will restore the disturbed internal balance to a state of equilibrium. The form of the behavior is not learned by the individual organism but is built into its structure so that it is an automatic, rigidly determined response to a particular disturbance of its internal state of equilibrium.

Man, far more complex than the amoeba and the spider, is still subject to that same principle of constancy, of dynamic physical-chemical equilibrium. No longer is it expressed in the primitive mechanism of tropism or in the complexly structured but still rigidly automatic behavior that we call instinct. Man has feelings, instead.

In my view, the capacity for feelings is part of a highly evolved system of adaptation. Feelings reflect our internal disequilibrium and impel us to action to restore internal balance. As disequilibrium is greater, our feelings will be more intense, creating a higher level of feeling tension that impels more strongly to action. That action, however, is not rigidly predetermined as it is in lower forms of life, and so there is far greater flexibility in man's system of adaptation. Feelings motivate man. They push toward action, but that action is neither peremptory nor fixed. Memory, judgment, and volition may intervene between the feeling and the action. The action can be delayed or even postponed indefinitely.

How long action can be delayed depends upon the particular internal disequilibrium that creates the feeling. If the feeling is hunger, the appropriate action can be delayed even for weeks when necessary, and the individual can still survive. If the feeling is thirst due to water imbalance, survival is measured in days. And if it is the feeling of suffocation due to lack of oxygen, survival is measured in only minutes. For these feelings, reflective of life-sustaining processes, variable delay is possible but appropriate action required to restore internal equilibrium is eventually mandatory for survival. Other feelings reflecting processes less fundamental to survival are still imperative. So, for example, Freud noted early in his writings that the moral restrictions placed upon man's sexuality lead often to illness (1908).

THREE CATEGORIES OF FEELINGS

Not all of our feelings, however, appear to be so easily related to our physiology. One can rather clearly see the connection of hunger, thirst, and sexual feelings to physical-chemical bodily processes, but there are many other feelings that strongly impel us to action and undeniably influence the direction of our lives, yet have no clearly apparent connection with our physiology. As examples, feelings of shame and guilt, loyalty and trust, have no relationship to our metabolic processes but appear to be directly related to our social interactions, instead. A feeling like hunger tends to be universal, manifesting itself in much the same way wherever man exists, but a feeling like shame appears to be far more subject to cultural influence. In some cultures the feeling of shame is more prevalent and significant than in others, and the conditions that evoke shame are most variable. In one culture the exposure of the naked body will evoke intense shame while in another nudity is taken for granted and evokes no shame at all. It is hard to ascribe a feeling like shame, then, to some fundamental physical-chemical process in all human beings.

This would appear to pose a problem for the view of feelings as reflections of internal disequilibrium, but only if we constrict our view of man to that of a complex physical-chemical system alone. That is essentially what Freud did when he asserted that feelings were always the psychic representations of physiologically based drives. This assertion created for us the improbable task of ascribing each in man's vast repertoire of feelings to a particular physiologically based drive or combination of drives. When this effort often failed, as it had to, psychologists' ingenuity invented hypotheses that treated feelings as though they were physical-chemical entities that could be fused, defused, and neutralized. These mental gymnastics and the confusion that they breed become unnecessary as we recognize that man's physical-chemical system is not his only system requiring the maintenance of equilibrium. His social system requires similar management.

The concept of drives has been, and continues to be, a useful one, but only if we clearly recognize that only some of man's feelings belong to those physiologically based processes that Freud called drives. Many other feelings arise as reflections of social disequilibrium, and again we can note some of the evolutionary antecedents of that aspect of man's adaptive capacity. The transition from tropism to instinct and then to feelings is only one of the features that marks the evolving complexity of life forms. Another significant feature on that scale is the appearance of interdependence between like organisms for the survival of the individual and for the perpetuation of its kind. The ant, the bee, the wolf, and the monkey came to live each in interdependent groups, and as the group is necessary for the survival of the individual, some manner of regulation of the group itself becomes mandatory. Equilibrium in these groups is maintained by instinctual behavior that determines territoriality, dominance, mating priorities, defense against attack, and cooperative food gathering. The degree to which these behaviors are rigidly built into the structure of the organism and the degree to which they may be learned is, perhaps, in doubt. Probably, the lower the evolutionary form of the organism, the more rigidly instinctual is its behavior. Higher life forms appear to display greater flexibility in the acquisition of these adaptational modes, but learned or in-built, the behavior tends to be rigidly stereotyped. In the more highly evolved human animal the corresponding process of social regulation is mediated again by feelings rather than by predetermined stereotyped behavioral responses.

"Social feelings" are not present at the beginnings of life. "Physiological feelings" like hunger and thirst are manifestly present from birth, but there is nothing in the behavior of the infant to suggest that feelings of shame and guilt, loyalty and trust, exist at that early time. It is only as the infant develops to the point of awareness of others, and awareness of his need of others, that social feelings emerge. Theirs is a later development and arise only as the need to maintain equilibrium in his social system becomes important to the child for his comfort and survival.

The development of this set of social feelings creates the stage for a fundamental conflict of feelings within the individual. Physiologically determined feelings are self-centered and asocial, serving to maintain equilibrium in the internal inter-acting systems of the individual. Social feelings serve to main-tain equilibrium in his social system which, due largely to man's prolonged period of relative helplessness and depen-dency through childhood, is equally important to his sur-vival. The conflict between individual and society is reflected in the internal conflict between those two sets of feelings, so often opposed in their goals.

And still we find that we have not yet embraced the full range of human feelings, for there are other feelings that resist classification as "physiological" or "social." The feeling of excitement, for example, has its own subjective quality, but does it derive from physiology or from social interaction? At first glance it appears to belong equally to both, for one can feel excitement in reference to sexual arousal, anger, grief, or guilt. Indeed, what characterizes the feeling of excitement is that it does not and cannot exist in and of itself but always arises in conjunction with some other feeling. It is a feeling that derives from feelings.

The feeling of excitement belongs to a third category of feelings which I shall call "signal feelings," borrowing the term from Freud. He used that term only in reference to anxiety (1926, p. 53), a feeling akin to fear that acts as a signal to inform us that a repressed (unconscious) thought or im-pulse is threatening to break through the repression barrier into our conscious awareness. I include within that "signal" category not only anxiety but all of those feelings that inform us about our social and physiological feelings. Because they inform us about the status of our social and physiogical feelings, signal feelings often have a special immediacy in determining our responses.

Excitement, then, is a signal feeling that attends the exis-tence of strong physiological or social feelings in conscious awareness which are close to discharge and action. Peace is the signal feeling that we experience when our physiological and social systems are essentially in equilibrium and no strong feelings are impelling us to action. Boredom is the signal feeling that indicates massive exclusion of feelings from conscious awareness. Pleasure and pain (unpleasure) are signal feelings that play a major motivating role in life but little agreement has been reached about how they arise and precisely what they signal.

The particular feelings mentioned above are meant only to exemplify the three categories; there is no assumption that they constitute a complete compendium of human affects. That would require an extensive work of its own. But all human feelings belong to these three categories: physiological feelings serving physiological equilibrium, social feelings serving social equilibrium, and signal feelings serving feeling equilibrium. Feeling states are often combinations of feelings of different categories, so one might feel sexual arousal (physiological), guilt (social), and excitement (signal) all together, yet it is important to know from where each of the feelings derives.

Another example of such complex feeling states involves our responses to art and music, to beauty in all its forms, but a clear discussion of those feelings would require a better understanding of aesthetics than we have available to us now.

What makes feelings so important to us is their impelling quality that moves us to action. Feelings are the primary motivating force in each of us. We often speak of the power of ideas and regard ideas as forces that shape people's lives, but there is some confusion in that. The force of an idea lies only in the strength of the feeling we have about that idea; an idea about which we feel nothing has no force at all. Ideas do give direction to our actions, but only feelings move us to action. Feelings are the motivator, ideas are the modifier.

TENSION AND THE CONSTANCY PRINCIPLE

The "internal milieu" of physiologist Claude Bernard and the principle of homeostasis of physician W. B. Cannon described the complex physiological interactions within the living organism that tend to maintain the organism's steady state. Freud's concept of the "constancy principle" was simply an extension of that idea to the psychological realm, proposing the existence of a "tendency to maintain intra-cerebral excitation at a constant level" (Studies on Hysteria, Breuer & Freud, 1895, 171ff).

Then in the human, each departure from equilibrium in his physiological or social systems is reflected in the mental sphere as a feeling, representing an increase in cerebral excitation. Feelings, therefore, always represent a departure from psychological equilibrium that impels the individual to action to restore equilibrium. As the responsible physiological or social disequilibrium is greater, so will its reflective feeling be more intense. It is here that we encounter the quantitative dimension in the realm of the mind. Psychology is often faulted for its failure to quantify its observations, but such quantification is an essential feature of psychology and goes on all of the time. More hungry or less hungry, more sexually aroused or less so, these are terms of measurement. They are not so precise as grams or centimeters, yet they are measurements of quantity nonetheless.

To deal more effectively with this quantitative dimension of mind we must bring in the concept of tension, a concept which has unfortunately developed a poor public reputation. Our advertising media floods us with slogans equating tension with headache and dyspepsia and exhorting us to stamp it out with a wide assortment of medications and prepaid vacations. So characterized, tension seems to be an avoidable evil, but it is not intrinsically evil and it most certainly is not avoidable. Tension is simply the experience of a departure from psychological equilibrium—that is, a departure from that mental state that we call peace. Tension is a subjective concomitant of every sensation and feeling, a measure of the stimulation of the mind. The stronger the sensation or feeling, the greater is the departure from psychological equilibrium and so the greater the tension, eventuating in that feeling that we call excitement.

Feelings and Tension

In physics, the term *tension* is defined as the stress of stretching an object and measures the force exerted by that object to return to its resting state. The mind is not a physical object and cannot be "bent out of shape" in any similar way, yet there is some reason that we use the same term to describe both a psychological experience and a physical phenomenon. The mind, in accordance with the constancy principle, is comparable to an object tending always toward return to its resting state. Tension, then, is the force exerted by a feeling or sensation toward discharge of excitation and the return to a resting mental state.

The prevalent negative association of tension with distress and discomfort comes from the particular circumstances of conflictual tension. In that situation a feeling is pressing toward discharge and action, but discharge is blocked by some prohibition of the feeling or the action. Restoration of equilibrium becomes impossible and tension mounts to unpleasurable levels. The discomfort is related not to tension itself, but to some excessive rise in tension. Pleasurable excitement and joy are tensions too, but they are not unpleasant.

Since man is subject to the constancy principle and is so sensitively attuned to disturbances in the equilibrium of his interacting systems, one might easily assume that the goal toward which he would constantly strive would be some enduring feeling of peace. Then, with physiological and social systems in relative equilibrium, there would be only small feelings and little tension pressing toward discharge in action. Such enduring states of blissful peace are rarely found, for social interactions and physiological needs quickly intrude. Perhaps one could pursue that goal by retreating from our usual social bedlam, becoming a hermit in ideal circumstances surrounded by plenty. A few have tried. Their success or failure in achieving enduring peace that way is quite beside the point. What is important is that so few have tried. Were enduring peace the ultimate goal of man, we should have expected a much more massive scramble along that path.

The fact is, man does not strive for the constant feeling of peace, but seeks pleasure instead. There is no contradiction here. The constancy principle, regulating complex interacting systems, is a biological force imposed upon us and is quite different from what we ourselves wish to experience. In a similar vein, gravity is a force of nature that keeps us earth-bound, yet we wish to fly and devise means to do so. When we observe people's behavior we are forced to conclude that equilibrium is not very high on their own list of priorities, for their search for pleasure leads them in directions directly opposed to equilibrium. The constancy principle tends toward peace, but man seeks pleasurable tensions.

PLEASURE AND PAIN (UNPLEASURE)

The "pleasure principle"—the search for pleasure and the avoidance of pain—was recognized by Freud to be a central motivation in all of us. The nature of pleasure and pain, the mechanisms by which these feelings arise, however, remains a crucial unresolved problem in psychology. Freud equated pleasure with decreasing tension, pain with increasing tension, but this formulation was never wholly satisfactory. It could not account for the pleasurable effect of rising tension in sexual foreplay or the pleasure of many other situations in which tension was heightened rather than lowered. Still, this formulation remains embedded in our theoretical structure, confounding understanding and demanding revision to avoid unresolvable paradoxes into which its errors lead us.

Pleasure and pain (or unpleasure) are always related to both sensation and feeling. Since we have already determined that every sensation and feeling is an excitation of the mind, a departure from that mental state of equilibrium that we call peace, it follows that every experience of pleasure and of pain accompanies a rise in tension. But if pleasure and pain are both characterized by heightened tension, then we must discover some mechanism by which we can distinguish between them for they certainly have very different effects.

Common usage places pleasure and pain in opposition to each other as though they occupy the two extremes on a continuum in which the middle range of excitation is indifferent, neither pleasurable nor painful. But another kind of relationship between pleasure and pain presents itself when we consider them in relation to physical sensations. Every physical stimulus that causes pain creates the feeling of pleasure when experienced in lower ranges of intensity. Intense heat and cold cause pain but mild warmth and coolness give rise to feelings of pleasure. Light touch is pleasurable but more intense pressure becomes painful. Pleasure and pain, then, do not occupy extremes on a continuum of excitation whose middle range is indifferent. Instead, they exist on a rising continuum of stimulus intensity in which the lowest levels of intensity are indifferent, the moderate levels are pleasurable, and the more intense levels are painful. This accords with our understanding that pain warns us of a threat to our physical integrity. There is a limit to the intensity of physical stimuli that our bodies can tolerate before being damaged, and pain warns of the approach of that limit.

I propose that a parallel exists in the realm of physiological feelings for there, too, the moderate ranges of intensity are pleasureable while higher extremes of intensity become unpleasureable. I use the rather clumsy term *unpleasure* rather than pain in the sphere of feelings because it approximates Freud's term *unlust,* which was originally mistranslated as "pain," and because that helps to maintain the important distinction between sensation and feeling. While social feelings are also pleasureable or unpleasureable, I find no evidence that the same relationship to intensity holds true. Social feelings are either pleasureable or unpleasureable in their entire range. There is no such thing as a low intensity of shame being pleasureable, for example, and that is probably because social feelings are related to learned cultural values and attitudes. Intensity only determines that a social feeling will be more or less pleasureable or more or less unpleasureable, depending on what feeling it is.

Hunger is an example of a physiological feeling that causes unpleasure only when it mounts to some critical level of intensity. In its milder form, hunger is known as appetite, and having a good appetite is, in and of itself, pleasurable. One might argue that the pleasure of appetite comes only through the anticipation of satisfying that hunger by eating, but anyone who has lost his appetite for a period of time knows the pleasure of its return. After all, the French salutary wish "Bon appetit," is certainly not meant as a curse upon the recipient.

And so it is with sexual desire, as well. The anticipation of sexual gratification adds an increment to the pleasure of feelings of sexual desire, but the feeling of sexual desire is pleasurable in and of itself. The tension of sexual feelings mounts during sexual foreplay and the feeling of pleasure rises in parallel, culminating in the climax of orgasm. The peace that follows orgasm reflects the return to psychological equilibrium after the discharge of excitation initiating the bodily responses that, together, comprise orgasm. But if sexual desire mounts to some critical level because the discharge of excitation is precluded for whatever reasons, then sexual tension becomes unpleasurable.

Threshold for Pain and Unpleasure

What, then, is the critical level of sensory-tension and feeling-tension that marks the transition from pleasure to pain and to unpleasure? We are quite familiar with the concept of a threshold for pain in the sensory sphere, a threshold that is known to be quite variable. Some people are said to have a very high tolerance for pain whereas others seem to have very little tolerance for it. What is meant by that is that some people can tolerate very high intensities of stimuli before experiencing the feeling of pain, while others experience the feeling of pain at much lower intensities. Not only is there variation among different individuals, but there are often wide variations in tolerance within the individual himself, at different times and under different circumstances. I suggest that a corresponding threshold for unpleasure exists in the realm of physiological feelings that is equally variable.

The factors that determine the variability of the thresholds for pain and for unpleasure are many. Constitutional endowment plays a role, but so may fatigue. The mother or father who delights in the noisy tumult of their childrens' play on a Sunday afternoon may come home after a hard and tiring Monday at work and find that very same tumult most unpleasurable. But there is far more involved than constitution and fatigue. Those who live with a high level of feeling tension because they are unable to acknowledge their feelings or because they are unable to appropriately discharge those tensions, may find that only a small added increment of tension is enough to push them over their thresholds. And those whose life experience has taught them, one way or another, to fear intensity within themselves will have low thresholds to defend against the consequences of their feared intensity.

How well we handle feeling-tension largely determines the success or failure of our lives. Those who function for themselves effectively and well, those who acknowledge the full range of their feelings and confidently trust their ability to discharge those tensions in appropriate and advantageous ways will have high self-esteem. They have achieved self-mastery and will tend to have high thresholds for pain and unpleasure, for they do not fear intensity and they will be able to experience the vitality that intense feelings bring to life.

3

Boredom, Anxiety, and Excitement: The Regulation of Tension

The tension of feelings is neither good nor bad, only inevitable. What makes that tension feel good or feel bad to the individual is determined by the location of that individual's threshold for unpleasure on the axis of rising tension. Those who have a high threshold are fortunate for they can enjoy high levels of pleasureable tension, while those with lower thresholds must limit the intensity of their pleasure lest it exceed their tolerance of tension and cause unpleasure instead. The dilemma must be seen clearly. We seek tension for its pleasureable effect, but only so much, for an added increment may push us over our edge and cause unpleasure.

We are constantly engaged, then, in a process of regulating our level of tension, usually without conscious recognition of the process for we each develop our own habitual or characteristic mode. Regardless of style, which is largely determined by life experience, we employ basically three psychic mechanisms for the regulation of tension: avoidance, psychic discharge, and repression. Each of these mechanisms carries its own, often hidden, costs. While we will be concerned with the costs of repression, anxiety and boredom, some preliminary statements about avoidance and psychic discharge are in order.

MECHANISMS OF REGULATION

Avoidance

Those with low thresholds for unpleasure must work often and hard to keep tension low. One way to accomplish this task is to avoid stimulation of the mind by strongly guarding against exposure to situations that might evoke intense feelings. However, the avoidance of life situations makes people withdrawn, constricted, and painfully shy; they lack a spirit of adventure, abhor risks, and avoid intimacy. They pay a high price for cold comfort.

Psychic Discharge

Another way to keep the level of tension low is by discharging any stimulation of the mind when stimulation occurs. This mechanism of the mind serves adaptation when the psychic discharge instigates action that is directed toward the restoration of equilibrium and removal of the source of the feeling that was stimulating the mind. But often the mechanism of psychic discharge, instigating action, is employed for its own sake, simply to get rid of tension, and the instigated action has no adaptive purpose. The latter mechanism is most manifest in the very young, for infants and young children, having little developed capacity for the containment of tension, respond quite automatically to their physiological feelings with those behaviors available to them; crying, sucking, and random movement. As their physiological feelings become more intense, their behaviors become correspondingly more vigorous. Although this mechanism for tension regulation is most clearly seen in the very young, it is by no means limited to them. Even adults who achieve a high level of self-containment often betray their original disposition through residual automatic behaviors like finger drumming, nail biting, or vigorous pacing, when experiencing the pressure of intense feeling.

Tension regulation by psychic discharge has its place in our repertoire, but its effectiveness is definitely limited. We must remember that a feeling reflects some disequilibrium within us and will continue as a tension so long as the disequilibrium persists. It is clear, then, that discharge and action for its own sake would have to be correspondingly continuous to be at all effective in regulating tension. Those youngsters of an earlier era who were counseled to run around the block to relieve sexual tension and thereby avoid the supposed evil of masturbation could attest to the sheer mileage such an effort required. Action instigated only for discharge, without direction toward restoration of equilibrium, leads only and inevitably to exhaustion. It may be a temporary means of lessening tension while an appropriate action is being determined and initiated. The agitated executive may decrease his tension for a time by his pacing, to better choose an advantageous course of action, but the pacing will not resolve the tension by itself.

Why, then, should we not always respond automatically with psychic discharge instigating action that is appropriate to the restoration of equilibrium? The answer is twofold. First, we are simply not so constructed. The amoeba, the spider, do respond that way, for the appropriate actions are built into their structures. Unlike them, we experience our feelings and then have to decide on a course of action. Yes, when we feel hungry we quite automatically know that eating is the appropriate action. But what to eat? Should we eat something already prepared, but cold? Should we cook up a fine meal, or should we go out to eat? The example may seem trivial, but it demonstrates the variety of decisions we must make about even so fundamental a feeling as hunger. The second part of the answer is more complex, for it involves our social relationships. An action that is appropriate to the restoration of internal equilibrium may create a social disequilibrium that is as intense or more intense than the one that the action was to repair. Eating may be the appropriate action to assuage hunger, but if the food immediately available belongs to another, eating it can lead to a great deal of difficulty.

Not only must we think about what action is appropriate to the feeling, but we must also consider what range of actions is acceptable within our social system. Then we must often choose which of the appropriate and acceptable actions is most advantageous. And all of this deliberation requires delay and the containment of tension.

There is no easy flight from tension. No wonder, then, that so many view feelings as a burden that complicates the living of their lives, and wish to be free of them. It's a futile wish, for there can be no life without feelings.

Repression

The complexity of the human mind provides another means of dealing with the burden of feelings in the mental mechanism of repression, which can block feelings from conscious awareness. It must be understood that the feeling that is repressed is not annihilated. It continues to exist, reflecting some disequilibrium within us, but is shut off from our conscious awareness. As long as the responsible disequilibrium exists, so does its reflective, now repressed, feeling persist, acting as a continuous psychic tension pressing toward consciousness and discharge in action. Because it is repressed, however, we cannot directly know the feeling or its tension, and that would seem to spare us the effort of deliberation and action that conscious feelings require. Still, we are not home free, for the consequences of repression of feelings can be very costly, as we shall see.

The precise mechanism by which repression works remains unknown, and we will probably have to wait for the neuro-physiologists to provide more information about the workings of the brain, the physical organ of the mind, to find the answer. What we do know is that the mind is capable of blocking feelings and thoughts from conscious awareness, and that this mechanism of repression proceeds quite unconsciously and automatically. However, we also know that repression is usually preceded by the conscious and voluntary act of *suppression* of the thought or feeling that subsequently becomes repressed. Strictly speaking, we cannot make a conscious volitional choice to repress a feeling or a thought, but we are able to push that feeling or thought out of our central focus of consciousness into some peripheral realm of the mind where the automatic process of repression takes over.

The most obvious problem with repression arises from the simple fact that since we can't know the repressed feeling, we remain uninformed of the underlying disequilibrium and deprived of an opportunity for active restitution. Further, the maintenance of repression requires the constant expenditure of mental effort, mental effort that might be better spent in coping with our often harsh external reality. And when the effort of repression threatens to fail, we are faced with the problem of anxiety, a very special case of tension that has been widely studied. Beyond that, I would add one more problem to the list, the cost to us of repression that is successful and extensive, the root of a little recognized but very prevalent psychopathological condition that I have termed chronic boredom (1975).

SIGNAL FEELINGS OF TENSION

Certain of our signal feelings have the explicit function of alerting us to our state of psychic tension; not only the degree of tension, but also its location within our psychic "apparatus." Three of those feelings, excitement, anxiety, and boredom, are of particular interest because their immediacy gives them an extremely significant role in determining the course of our lives.

Freud recognized early the central significance of anxiety. He and his followers studied it extensively, describing its mechanism and its varied manifestations, so little further elaboration of that signal feeling will be required here. The signal feeling of excitement, accessible as it is to conscious awareness, will also need only brief elaboration. Mainly we will examine in detail the signal feeling of boredom and its various ramifications.

Boredom deserves extensive attention for two reasons. First, it is a most significant, widespread, and unpleasurable feeling in its own right that has been little recognized and even less understood, despite the prevalence of the misery it creates. Understanding its mechanism and its ramifications for the possible therapeutic advantage that that might afford would be a worthy goal in itself. But, beyond that, the condition of chronic boredom, by its very nature, creates an opportunity to observe the effects of the exclusion of feelings from conscious awareness, informing us of many hitherto unrecognized aspects of the vital importance of experiencing our feelings consciously.

Excitement

Excitement, being "stirred up," is the signal feeling that attends the experience of strong physiological and social feelings in conscious awareness. It is the conscious experience of being strongly impelled toward action by high feeling tension. When excited we must move; we jump for joy, moan our despair and our grief, stomp with rage. We must move, no matter how we strive to contain our tension. Even if we permit ourselves no other movement, then we tremble or quiver with excitement. No wonder that so many are fearful of excitement. It is the narrow edge between our capacity for self-containment and action with all of its social consequences. We cannot contain the tension to carefully deliberate our course of action; our action bursts forth. And so at the least we reveal ourselves to others and we risk their displeasure if our impulsive action turns out to be unacceptable to them.

Excitement itself has no pleasure/unpleasure dimension, but refers only to the height of feeling tension. That does not mean that the excited individual experiences no pleasure or no unpleasure; he will experience one or the other. Sexual excitement may be extremely pleasurable, while excitement with grief will be most unpleasurable. But excitement relates only to the extremity of feeling tension, whereas pleasure/unpleasure relates to the specific feeling involved and to the intensity of that feeling in relationship to that individual's threshold for unpleasure at that specific time. Even the prevalent fear of excitement is not a property of excitement. That person whose childhood excitement was met by parental disapproval will tend to be more fearful of it than one whose childish excitement was greeted with parental pleasure.

Excitement is always a strain on our mental capacities, even in its most pleasurable forms. We want pleasurable excitement and strive to experience it repeatedly, but because of its very nature it cannot be long maintained. It impels discharge and action and a return toward equilibrium. The lower the threshold for unpleasure, the greater is the avoidance of excitement, for fear of the unpleasurable consequences of high levels of feeling tension. For those people who cannot tolerate excitement, the course is avoidance and isolation, or repression of feeling.

Anxiety

As we have seen, the repression of feelings does not relieve us of the tension of those feelings, but it does remove those

Boredom, Anxiety, and Excitement: The Regulation of Tension

feelings from conscious awareness, thereby relieving us of the need to determine our action. Since we do not consciously know the feeling, we cannot know the direction of appropriate action. Still, the tension of the feeling persists and presses toward consciousness and discharge, instigating action, which is the usual route of feeling-tension. Since the path toward consciousness is blocked, the feeling-tension seeks an aberrant pathway to discharge. There are a number of alternatives. If the feeling-tension is moderate and the individual's capacity for repression is strong, the tension may be contained below conscious awareness or it may be continuously discharged in a generalized way, creating those all too numerous people who appear to us to be excessively tense, yet who profess to know nothing of the cause of their tenseness.

There are some theories, not finally proven but worthy of continued investigation, that various "psychosomatic" illnesses, such as peptic ulcer, asthma, and specific types of arthritic disease, are the ultimate expression of that kind of generalized unconscious discharge of feeling-tension. Another aberrant path to discharge may take the form of sudden breaks in the repressing barrier, allowing the repressed feeling to burst forth in the unconscious blunders, or parapraxes, described by Freud (1901)—i.e., slips of the tongue, symptomatic acts, etc.

The problem with repression is that since the disequilibrium that is the source of the feeling-tension remains unresolved, the feeling-tension persists and the effort of repression must be continuously maintained. If the feeling-tension mounts or, conversely, if the effort of repression begins to fail, then the established balance becomes threatened and the signal feeling of anxiety is experienced. Anxiety, akin to the feeling of fear, signals the threatened failure of repression, the danger from within of the emergence into consciousness of a forbidden or unwanted feeling and its tension.

It is probably worth a moment's time to reemphasize the distinction between fear and anxiety, terms which are all too often erroneously interchanged. Fear is the specific feeling we experience when we encounter a known external danger. Anxiety, a feeling that is subjectively experienced very like the feeling of fear, arises when there is a threat from within, when a repressed feeling threatens to break into conscious awareness. But that forbidden feeling is still repressed and not consciously known, and therefore anxiety differs from fear in that anxiety lacks a specific focus. In anxiety there is a feeling of foreboding, a sense of unknown danger. Therefore it is incorrect, for example, to speak of anxiety about nuclear war. That's a fear, real and external. The person who is truly *anxious* about a nuclear explosion is poetically describing his vague sense of danger of an internal explosion of feeling.

Anxiety, like fear, is a most unpleasurable feeling and mobilizes all of our available defenses. Freud early realized the central role of anxiety in the development of the neuroses and most of his work was directed to the elucidation of that area of psychology. In brief summary, he taught us that anxiety, signaling the threatened failure of repression, mobilized first a stronger effort of repression, but if that failed, then secondary mechanisms of defense were brought into play. Then such mechanisms as displacement, condensation, substitution of a part for the whole, etc., created disguised pathways for the discharge of forbidden feeling-tensions in the form of neurotic symptoms (1915b).

There is another confusion of terms also requiring clarification. Anxiety is not only confused with fear but is also frequently equated with tension. Anxiety is only one manifestation of tension, but excitement is also a manifestation of tension and, as I shall attempt to demonstrate, boredom is another.

Boredom

Freud proposed that repression, since it exists outside of conscious awareness, could not be directly known but could only be recognized by its failure—i.e., by parapraxes or by the anxiety that attended its threatened failure. That view has been quite consistently held by psychologists since then. My own view is in part at variance, for I believe that we can also know repression by its success, through the boredom that results when repression of feeling is extensive and successful. These are the circumstances that create "chronic boredom".

This is not the conventional or usual view of boredom, which tends to hold the external world responsible—if I am bored then something out there is boring me. Were our world a dull and dreary place, boredom might be explicable on that basis, but how then would we account for the prevalence of boredom in an exciting world? Amid unprecedented affluence, personal freedom to match, and a technology that crowds our time with exciting, sometimes frightening, advances and innovations, boredom has become a serious obstruction to the search for happiness in a great many lives. Plainly, people would prefer to place the blame outside because chronic boredom has acquired a demeaning connotation. The person who is often or always bored is frequently dismissed as trivial and unworthy, reflecting some idiosyncratic flaw of shallowness and superficiality. Yet one need only look about to recognize the seriousness of the psychopathology of chronic boredom to realize its cost to many lives.

Some few thinkers in the past have recognized boredom as a formidable force. Nietzsche, for example, said, "Against boredom even the gods themselves struggle in vain" (1964). And Dostoevsky reflected, "Of course boredom may lead you to anything. It is boredom sets one sticking golden pins into people" (1960). But for most, the very real problem of boredom is only recently coming to be recognized, still distorted by old prejudice and clouded by our inadequate understanding of the role of feelings in our lives.

Boredom versus "Chronic Boredom"

We must distinguish the feeling of boredom from the psychopathological condition of chronic boredom, even though the *feeling* of boredom is paramount in the latter. We are more familiar with this distinction in reference to other feelings and their related pathological feeling states. One parallel may be seen in the distinction between fear and anxiety, another in that between grief and depression. Fear is an appropriate feeling in the presence of an external danger. When fear is present all or much of the time, without reference to any explicit external danger, we recognize that feeling to be a reflection of an internal dysfunction and we call it anxiety. Grief is an appropriate feeling response to the loss of a valued person or object, but when grief is present without reference to any real loss, we call that state depression. The feeling of boredom, like fear and grief, is an emotional response to a real (external) situation; chronic boredom, like anxiety and depression, is the expression of an internal psychological disturbance.

What then is the real (external) situation that evokes the signal feeling of boredom? It is any circumstance that requires the massive exclusion of physiological and social feelings from conscious awareness. It is a transient feeling that lasts only as long as that requirement is in effect, and as soon as we can again allow ourselves conscious awareness of our feelings, the feeling of boredom quickly dissipates. So when trapped by an after-dinner speaker who has little to say, and says it poorly, the dictates of polite society demand that we not reveal our true feelings. We sit there and pay attention and feel bored. But those of us (and we are large in number) who have mastered the technique of only appearing to listen while actually retreating into reverie are able to quickly dissipate our boredom by enjoying all of the feelings that accompany our fantasied exploits, romantic or heroic. Of course the student in a classroom may not be so fortunate for he may get marked down for his lack of attention, and the punch-press operator knows that he may lose life or limb if he gives himself up to reverie. They must endure the feeling of boredom for longer periods but they, too, are eventually freed from the requirement of excluding feelings and their boredom then disappears.

In these instances the feeling of boredom is transient, for the exclusion of feelings from conscious awareness is accomplished by suppression, which is a conscious and volitional act that we can impose upon ourselves in varying degrees and then suspend, as circumstances and judgment demand. When, however, the exclusion of feelings from conscious awareness is accomplished by repression, instead, we have a very different situation. Repression is an unconscious act outside of volitional control. Once established, we cannot remove it at will. And when repression of feelings is extensive and successful, then the boredom so created is no longer transient and related to particular external circumstance. It has become an internal and continuous dysfunction, chronic boredom.

The *feeling* of boredom is the same whether it be the result of suppression or of repression. What is different is the location of the cause and the constancy of the feeling in chronic boredom. Perhaps it is the sameness of the feeling that makes it easy for the chronically bored to come to the unhappy and mistaken conclusion that theirs is a boring world, for they confuse the feeling of boredom with the malaise of chronic boredom. Since they always feel bored, it is a small step for them to conclude that all they encounter is boring.

THE MALAISE OF CHRONIC BOREDOM

It is difficult to think of many things more difficult to endure than constant and unending boredom. "Bored to death," "bored to tears," "bored to distraction," are common descriptive phrases that provide a glimpse of both the variety of its effects and the intensity of its discomfort. Anyone who can recall his last experience of boredom, transient though it may have been, will surely acknowledge the discomfort of that feeling, and he will readily understand that the person who suffers chronic boredom will resort to almost any means

Boredom, Anxiety, and Excitement: The Regulation of Tension

to be rid of it. Boredom is a feeling for which we have but a very limited tolerance, and anyone forced to endure boredom all or much of the time will be pressed to use his ingenuity to the utmost to find ways to escape. And those are two of the fundamental reasons that chronic boredom has so long escaped explicit recognition, despite its prevalence, its cost in human suffering, and its quite specific psychodynamic cause. Its manifestations are most varied, and its picture is usually further obscured by the victim's desperate and usually misguided effort toward self-cure.

First we must approach the condition of chronic boredom, itself, to assess its essential features unobscured by individual restitutive efforts. It is difficult to draw upon past references in literature to help us with the task because the specific distinction between boredom as a feeling and chronic boredom as a malaise has not been drawn before. Yet psychoanalysis has not entirely ignored the subject of boredom. Dr. R. R. Greenson provides us with a description of boredom that we can profitably use as a starting point:

> The uniqueness of the feeling of being bored seems to depend upon the coexistence of the following components: a state of dissatisfaction and a disinclination to action; a state of longing and an inability to designate what is longed for; a sense of emptiness; a passive, expectant attitude with the hope that the external world will supply the satisfaction; a distorted sense of time in which time seems to stand still. (1963)

I accept this as an apt and useful description of the feeling of boredom, and since the feeling of boredom is the same whether it be a transient feeling response or the manifestation of the internal dysfunction of chronic boredom, it will be all the same to us. I would only add that Greenson, in his article, follows the lead of Fenichel (1934) and other earlier psychoanalytic writers in describing what appears to be two forms of boredom, a restless or agitated boredom and an apathetic boredom. With this latter view I cannot agree for, as Greenson's own statement above indicates, restlessness and apathy always coexist in boredom. Indeed, it is the coexistence of these two seemingly incongruous tendencies that makes chronic boredom so varied in its manifestations, and therefore difficult to recognize as a specific psychopathological entity.

The "state of dissatisfaction" refers to the restlessness, the "disinclination to action" to the apathy; depending upon which is predominant, the specific manifestations will vary, but these are not two different forms of boredom. One may dominate the picture in one person's boredom while the other may dominate the next, or their dominance may alternate within one person, but restlessness and apathy are always present together to some degree in boredom.

One significant feature of boredom that is omitted in Greenson's description is the characteristic lack of interest and the difficulty in paying attention that always attends a lack of interest. It is self-evident that one lacks interest in things when one is bored, yet this observation is not superfluous. The capacity to be interested is an internal matter and not the exclusive function of things out there. Although it is true that one may find oneself in circumstances in which there is nothing out there to arouse and attract one's interest, the capacity to feel interested is an internal function susceptible to internal interference. Unless we are clear about this we can be misled by the chronically bored person's mistaken notion that he feels interest in nothing simply because nothing is interesting. We might as well accept a blind man's notion that he sees nothing because there is nothing to see.

The sense of emptiness is a constant finding in chronic boredom, but Greenson's attempted explanation for it remains problematical. In his terms it represents a "stimulus hunger," a restless craving for stimulation. Yet I may attend a concert that fully engages my interest—I am not bored at all—while my neighbor occupying the next seat is extremely bored receiving the very same stimulation. The music is no louder for me than for him; there is no more stimulus for one than the other. It is not the lack of stimulation that accounts for the emptiness, but the lack of conscious feeling about the stimulus that explains the difference in the bored person. And the undesignated longing in each bored person is the wish to be *full of feeling* once more. Yet, in another sense Greenson is quite right in ascribing a "stimulus hunger" to the chronically bored, for their behavior clearly reveals that they often search most vigorously for stimulation. What is involved is the bored person's misdirected attempt to replace the emptiness of feelinglessness with the fullness of sensation. We shall examine that problem in greater detail a bit later.

The feeling of emptiness, reflecting the absence of feelings in conscious awareness, is accompanied by another phenomenon that I can only describe as a sense of "hollowness," a lack of substantiality or of authenticity, reflecting some interference with the usually constant and continuous sense of self. It is this sense of hollowness that leads many of the chronically bored to think of themselves as phonies or facades, as pretend people who walk through their roles as actors might do in preparation for a play. They have the impression that they are never fully participants in life but always observers of the passing scene, watching it all happen as though from some distant vantage point.

Alienation is the term that has gained currency to describe this sense of distance and isolation, this experience of separation from others. But alienation is more than a social phenomenon referring to the relationship between people. It ultimately derives from the individual's experience of not being wholly in touch with himself, of being cut off from an essential aspect of his own existence. It is the expression of the individual's incapacity to fully experience his own feelings with directness and intensity. And when man is alienated from himself, it is inevitable that he will be secondarily alienated from his fellows, for if he cannot know his own feelings he certainly will be unable to be empathically in touch with others.

The inability to experience one's own feelings directly and intensely is the root of chronic boredom. Apathy, literally translated, means "without feeling," and although we are not often enough mindful of it, it is the experience of feelings that gives to life its liveliness, its meaningfulness, its zest. Being interested is always and only an expression of feeling. One is interested in food only when one *feels* hungry; one is interested in sex only when one *feels* sexual desire; one is interested in exploration only when one *feels* curiosity. There can be no interest without feeling. The sense of emptiness, too, is an expression of the lack of consciously experienced feeling, and the unspecified restless longing is to fill that aching emptiness within one's self, to be full of feeling once more.

Usually the pressure of restless dissatisfaction and longing predominates in chronic boredom, interspersed with shorter periods in which apathetic resignation becomes the dominant mood. When apathy is predominant for long periods of time, that person has reached the level of despair. He has given up the fight and sees himself forever trapped in the numbed unfeelingness of his existence. This comprises the specific depression of chronic boredom, the grieving for the lost hope of achieving liveliness. Although its mechanism has remained unrecognized, it is probably the most common form of depression encountered. Its consequences are most serious, creating in many the conviction that life is not worth living, and leading thence to suicide, especially but not exclusively in the young. In this depressive state the depression is recognized, of course, but the central part that boredom plays in it is missed, and so the depression is misunderstood in terms of chemical imbalances or familial tendencies, or dynamically it is forced to fit the procrustean frame of melancholic depression with its guilt and its rage turned back upon the self. But we shall deal more extensively with the specific depression of boredom in the next chapter.

Restitutive Efforts of the Chronically Bored

As long as the restless dissatisfaction predominates, the struggle to achieve feelingfulness goes on. What we as observers often see in the chronically bored, then, is not the direct expression of boredom itself but the obscuring secondary manifestations of the frantic and desperate efforts to find relief from their misery. These restitutive efforts are most diverse, and often most strenuous. That those vigorous efforts frequently lead from one kind of misery to another is cannily described by Camus in the following passage from his novel *The Fall* (1956):

> I knew a man who gave twenty years of his life to a scatter-brained woman, sacrificing everything to her, his friendships, his work, the very respectability of his life, and who one evening recognized that he had never loved her. He had been bored, that's all, bored like most people. *Hence he had made himself out of whole cloth a life full of complications and drama.* Something must happen—and that explains most human commitments. *Something must happen, even loveless slavery, even war or death.* [Italics added]

For the chronically bored, something must happen. Boredom may lead them to anything. Their restitutive efforts go mainly in two directions: either they attempt to replace their missing feelings with sensations, or they attempt to create situations that will evoke feelings of such intensity that those feelings will break through their repressing barriers into conscious awareness. Apparently in response to this growing search for sensation, our literature and cinema tend toward ever more startling and shocking impacts, portraying sex and violence in increasingly graphic detail under the guise of realism; contemporary music favors the fundamental emphatic rhythms of hard rock played at ear-splitting volumes; the graphic arts aspire to shock by the use of vivid and discordant colors, unexpected and unusual materials, and startling contents. Sex, of course, is a ubiquitous source of sensation, and we may suspect that the present wide acceptance of casual sex is not so much an initiating revolution in morals as it is a consequence of the search for sensation in the absence of feelings. Eating is another accessible activity to provide sensations and, in my experience, most snackers and episodic gorgers are at least secretly aware of the correlation between their overeating and their boredom. The list of such distractive activities is extensive.

When the restitutive efforts of the chronically bored go in the direction of a search for feelings, they often become thrill seekers. They may take to motorcycle racing or downhill skiing, and if that isn't enough, they can turn to skydiving. Stepping out of an airplane with a parachute strapped to your back is apt to evoke enough fear to break through almost any degree of boredom. Of course, we periodically hear of people engaging in such activities encountering severe, sometimes fatal accidents, and far too often those people are considered to be self-destructive. Sometimes they are truly so, but probably more often they are not. Even though self-destruction is the consequence of their actions, it is not the purpose of those actions, for the thrill seekers out of boredom find themselves in a difficult dilemma: Their activity must be sufficiently challenging to evoke fear, but once they have mastered that activity the fear diminishes and the risk has to be escalated. The motorcycle must go ever faster over ever more rough terrain and eventually the risk exceeds their competence, and an accident occurs. It looks like self-destruction is their purpose, but often it is only the escalating effort to overcome boredom.

It is difficult to comprehend that some would court the unpleasurable feeling of fear, and yet we know that they do. Clearly, they find it more desirable to feel even fear than to endure the unfeeling emptiness of boredom. And so it is with pain and unpleasure as well. Those who court pain and unpleasure are frequently mislabeled masochistic, but again their purpose is not to suffer, but to break their boredom. It is paradoxical that those who have sought most energetically to avoid fear, pain, and unpleasure by erecting repression barriers to exclude their feelings from consciousness, now vigorously search for fear, pain, and unpleasure as preferable to their self-created boredom.

Alcohol, "mind-expanding" drugs, "uppers" and "downers" have gained widespread use, again to intensify sensation or to chemically weaken the internal barriers against feelings. And, at a different level, the growth in popularity of the "encounter" therapies attests to the restless search for feeling, for the avowed purpose of these therapies is to increase the feeling experience of their members.

Given this brief and rather sketchy overview of the behavior of the chronically bored, it is small wonder that the variety of chronic boredom has so long escaped recognition as expressive of a single psychopathological entity with a common dynamic cause. The chronically bored seem to be most vigorous people—sensation seekers, thrill seekers, masochists, sexual gymnasts, gourmands—when not apathetic and depressed. We find it difficult to think that vigorous people are bored for we assume that vigorous activity is the expression of strong feelings. That assumption is not wholly accurate. Some people behave vigorously because they feel strongly, but others behave vigorously in an effort to feel something—to feel almost anything at all.

Midlife Crisis

The picture of chronic boredom becomes even more varied as we consider its different manifestations in different age groups. In the middle-aged group its most common manifestation is that syndrome we have come to call midlife crisis. Here the restless dissatisfaction, the emptiness, and the longing, usually come to conscious awareness in people in their forties or fifties. Often these people sense that something is missing from their lives and, in typical fashion, they search for external explanations for their disappointment, calling into question their careers, their marriages, and even their geography. The lawyer thinks she would have been happier as a doctor, the advertising executive speculates that he should have been a farmer, the housewife concludes that she made a terrible mistake in cutting her education short and in not pursuing a commercial career of her own. Some actually change careers at this time while others throw themselves back into established careers with greater vigor, simply believing that they have not accomplished enough. Some seek to resolve the problem by changing their geography, moving their homes to one or another fantasied Shangri-La. Each secretly or loudly accuses his spouse of being boring. He believes that if she were brighter, sexier, more capable of sharing his interests, life would be good. She believes that if he were more aggressive, more successful, more attentive, more romantic, life would fulfill her expectations. Often both seek their solutions in secret sexual affairs, each believing the other to be sexually uninterested and uninteresting. Divorce and remarriage become ever more common. But what has really happened is that their long-latent chronic boredom has finally become revealed. Failing to identify the internal source of their own distress, they blame each other or the external conditions of their lives.

In actuality, the conditions for their chronic boredom were present long before, but its manifestations were masked by the intense distractive activity of youth and young adulthood, just as in a man with a toothache whose house is on fire, the toothache remains unnoticed until he and and his family are moved to safety and his home is rescued from the flames. Only then, with life made secure, does he become aware of the toothache that was present but unnoticed before, and the dull aching pain now becomes unbearable.

For the chronically bored middle-aged, youth was spent in intensive preparation for adulthood and career and if boredom was manifest from time to time, it was conveniently countered by the optimism of youth that clings to the hope that things will get better in time. Early marriage was a busy time, establishing a home, a family, a career, a social position. By middle age the distractive defense against boredom begins to unravel. Financial and social position have usually been established by then, and a degree of comfort and security have been achieved. The children are usually grown and perhaps most or all of them have left home. Now there is no need for extra jobs just to make ends meet, no more frantic midnight calls to the pediatrician. Now there is only the well-earned peace and leisure long anticipated. But unfortunately, they have been operating under the illusion that life would come later, that through earlier diligence, restraint, and postponement, the preparatory work would be done, ensuring the good life at some future time. They arrive at middle age with a degree of comfort and ease but without joy or happiness, and time is running out so they can no longer cling to that optimistic hope that time, alone, will make the difference. The distractive defense is gone, and their chronic boredom comes to the surface.

Chronic Boredom in the Young

Some cannot make it to middle age before their chronic boredom becomes manifest. Recent decades have witnessed the spread of chronic boredom in manifest form to large numbers of the young. Again, the picture is most varied, for the youth culture has developed its own distinctive styles of distraction. For those now middle-aged, the distractive style consisted largely of sneaky sex, alcohol, and the struggle for profit and position. The young have their own modes. Some drop out and, of those, some turn to the mystic religions of the Far East or the far out, while others seek a return to the simple life, forming communes to live in a semblance of earlier rural times. Some do battle and some do sex. Some take drugs and others take trips. But underneath the manifold variety of behaviors there lies the consistent thread of a search for vitality, for the energetic experience of feeling fully alive.

In the 1960s the rising incidence of college dropouts became a social phenomenon, and many universities responded by adopting the policy of granting leaves of absence to students who felt some need to "find themselves." Occasional college dropouts had always existed before, but these were different, for their motivation was not financial hardship, family requirement, or simple inability to make the grade. Very often they were from upper middle class socioeconomic backgrounds and had demonstrated their academic proficiency by excellent records through primary and secondary schools. They did not claim that the work was too hard but that the universities offered nothing of interest.

That was an awesome thought! Most of us have our own ideas about improvements that such institutions could make, but the notion that in the vast resources of leading universities bright young people could find nothing of interest seemed startling. The truth became revealed, however, as one pursued the matter further to discover that these young people were not only uninterested in what the universities had to offer, but they were also largely uninterested in anything else. No change by the university could alter the crippled internal capacity for interest of those young people.

The college dropout was declaring himself to be unwilling to commit himself to a choice. To go on required that decisions be made about which road he wished to follow. Unable to be interested in any of the roads before him, therefore unable to feel any conviction about which road to take, he wished to make that dimension of time stand still and he declared a moratorium. He had witnessed the terrible cost of commitment without interest and conviction in his parents' generation, and he struggled against repeating their mistake.

The young also became very involved in the "drug scene" during this period, and that continues as a source of concern and alarm. Many of their elders accused them of escapism or considered them to be the spoiled brats of affluence, given too much too soon by a permissive society and therefore lacking the moral fiber to work for goals and to postpone gratification. But there need be little mystery about the real reason for drug abuse by the young if one is only willing to listen to their own explanation. Quite uniformly they say that they take drugs because it makes them feel good. It "expands" their minds, intensifies their awareness of sensation and feeling, makes them feel more alive. If that is escapism, it is a wish to excape only the dull unfeelingness of their constant boredom. Of course it is unfortunate that they choose a means to liveliness that is so potentially harmful, and that is an unhappy expression of their desperation about experiencing intensity of feeling without resort to such dangerous artificial means.

During the sixties young people also turned to confrontation. Those were the days of campus unrest—when riots, protests, and an open thwarting of sexual and political conventions had become the norm. It was a loud and active period, fraught with danger and spotted with tragedy. While some view the student movement of the 1960's as a time of courageous protest for necessary reform, others would be more inclined to agree with Frederick Crews who characterized their movement as "dissatisfaction in search of issues." (1972) There is, in my opinion, some truth to both of these views and it is important to our present discussion of chronic boredom to sort out the issues involved.

Certainly there were plenty of social issues of legitimate and pressing concern during the sixties. Yet while some students were moved to join the activists by a desire to change the world, others were drawn to the movement by a desire to go where the action was. And just as drugs hold out the promise of heightened stimulation, confrontation holds out the promise of an intense involvement that can relieve the symptoms of chronic boredom. The latter group, drawn by the promise of community, excitement, even danger, were getting involved not only for reasons of social conscience but also to fill a personal void. For these individuals, no matter how earnest their efforts to effect reform in the universities, in governmental policies, and in the very fabric of traditional American society, their involvement could never succeed in bringing about the sense of fulfillment they were seeking. For them, even when positive changes were wrought, this would do little to ease their discontent since no amount of external change could satisfy their deep yearning to feel more fully alive.

The student protests of the sixties revealed a generation earnestly struggling for greater personal autonomy, but that worthy inner goal became obscured by the indiscriminate battles with every and any form of external authority. Still, we should not sell short the value of battle for battle's sake, for it can serve a very important function for the chronically bored. A cause, especially one that has clear ethical justification, has great intrinsic value, for it may evoke intense feelings in individuals who are not ordinarily capable of feeling very much. All the better if standing up for a cause means the promise of confrontation, since battle strikes the sparks of liveliness so ardently desired by the chronically bored. It is an unhappy fact that battle makes the bored feel more alive. There is danger to evoke fear, aggression that justifies aggression, and in the heat of battle there can also be love for a fellow comrade in arms felt with an intensity that quickly evaporates when the battle is done. One must never underestimate the importance of battle to the chronically bored, for few other circumstances have such capacity to evoke strong feelings.

Though the outward manifestation of their chronic boredom has moderated since the sixties, the underlying condition persists in today's youth. Perhaps the fierce and sometimes bloody examples of oppression that punctuated the late sixties, and the severe "law and order" reaction of the seventies, have intimidated the youth of today into apparent conformity and compliance, and their preferred modes of distraction assume the coloration of their stronger, more powerful elders. Certainly the so-called "Yuppies" of the eighties seem at first glance altogether different from the younger generation of the sixties and seventies. Yet upon closer inspection the difference is largely superficial. Today's youth have not abandoned drugs—they have simply switched brands. Alcohol consumption has increased as the use of marijuana has decreased; cocaine has usurped the place of

LSD. Their battlefield has moved to the grain pits, the option exchanges, and the mortgage banks, away from the college campuses, political conventions, and seats of government. They have discarded the political route to self-realization in favor of the avid pursuit of wealth. Instead of trying to create change by direct confrontation with their elders, they are deposing their elders by beating them at their own game. Because the conventions are no longer being thwarted outright it even appears that the youth have returned to the "old game"—sneaky sex, alcohol, and the struggle for profit and position. Hence, the young are thought by some to have finally returned to their senses and to have found contentment in the American Dream of old. Yet the colorful array of very expensive high-tech toys, like the emblematic political armbands of the 60s and 70s, will carry our youth only so far.

The Roots of Chronic Boredom

No matter what age group chronic boredom appears in, the cause is always a massive repression of feeling. Such repression is not sudden, appearing without prior history at age fifty or at age twenty. It is a process that begins early in life, a part of the individual's character defense development. And its development is influenced by a wide range of factors and circumstances. For example, a young child who loses a parent through death or divorce, lacking an accurate conceptual understanding of that event, may blame his own ambivalent feelings toward that parent for the loss. He develops a repressive defense against his feelings lest those feelings arise again to cause another calamitous loss. Another child may be brutalized by pathologically strict and rigid parents who will brook no disturbance caused by the noise of excitement, and he will defend against feelings to secure his survival. These and other extreme but occasional conditions can be the root of chronic boredom but, in my experience, the far more prevalent cause of chronic boredom is to be found in the premature socialization of children by parents who are too zealous in their efforts to prepare their children for success. These parents fail to recognize the child's need for time for emotional development, even while being aware of the time required for intellectual and physical development. Children must *learn* to manage their feelings, just as they must learn to manage their bodies. Instead, they are trained too early to behave in socially acceptable ways.

This refers not simply to toilet training, which may be only a small part of the broader behavioral coercion. They are trained to be polite, to be subdued, to share with other children, to be patient, to get along. In short, the theory appears to be that social success depends upon the development of proper adult behavior and the child who can master those techniques early has a head start toward achieving the goal. What is wrong with the theory is that it leaves the child's feelings out of account and the child becomes a "little man" or a "little lady" whose behavior is disconnected from his feelings. Thus deprived of childhood, they grow large and mimic adult behavior, while their repressed feelings remain those of the very young child. They don't *feel* polite, sharing, cooperative, but merely act as if they do.

Training is a process that ignores the feelings of the subject. Its goal is a certain behavior, like it or not. Most children can be trained to comply with the demand for social behavior if that training is sufficiently rigorous. It results in a form of learning, but one that is far inferior to the optimal kind of learning of which the human being is capable. Training leads to rigidity of behavior and requires the exclusion of feelings. Then, like a circus animal trained to sit upright upon a chair, the child can perform social tricks, but he is not doing what comes naturally.

There is a vast difference between the control of feelings achieved by repression and the control achieved through the process of learning to manage and contain tensions. If we were to speak of controlling horses instead of feelings, two comparable approaches could be conceived. One could ride a lot and through that extended experience become familiar with the nature of the beast, learning in time how to control and direct its energy, its power. But that involves the arduous task of learning—the beginner's fear, the bumps and bruises, the occasional falls that one might well expect to be a part of that experience. Or one might simply opt to keep the horse forever locked in the barn. The second approach would certainly guarantee control over the horse, but at the expense of rendering oneself a pedestrian throughout life. You thereby avoid the pain of being thrown, the danger of a runaway, but you sacrifice the exhilarating experience of horse and rider working synchronously.

So it is with our feelings. The child, given adequate time and support, can learn to manage his feelings by becoming thoroughly familiar with them. By thus familiarizing himself, the child will gradually learn to "ride" with his feelings, gaining confidence over time that he can master their unexpected twists and turns. Yet only by being allowed this opportunity to find his way around his feelings will the child learn how best to cope with his tensions, and discover appropriate ways to discharge them. The child who is not allowed sufficient time to be a child is forced to cut himself off from his feelings in order to comply behaviorally with the demands placed upon him from without. He learns to be a little adult— he learns it by rote. An introduction means, "How do you do?" A joke means you smile politely. Age twenty or twenty-five means that you look for someone to marry. Marriage means that you act like you love someone. But such an adult is likely to feel nothing, because feelings blocked by repression early in life tend to remain blocked from experience. Such people often become exquisitely sensitive clue seekers, their antennae ever alert for clues to appropriate behavior. This is necessary because they have lost touch with their internal clues to behavior—their feelings. They feel empty— empty of feeling—and therefore insubstantial. They have become "adapted" members of society at the cost of a crushing chronic boredom.

4

Chronic Boredom: The Quiet Desperation

"The mass of men lead lives of quiet desperation. . . . A stereotyped but unconscious despair is concealed even under what are called the games and amusements of mankind."
—*Thoreau (1854)*

Discontent has many roots, many causes, and chronic boredom is but one of its several forms. Without an understanding of the causes and the mechanisms of that discontent, there is little to do but curse the fates or accept it as part of the "human condition," whatever is meant by that. Psychoanalysis has revealed the meaning in large areas of human misery since Freud first opened that door to understanding, and many things formerly accepted with passive resignation are so accepted no more. Still, discontents persist that we continue to ascribe to a mysterious, undefined, "human condition." There is more to be understood.

As we have seen, the prevalence of chronic boredom has remained largely unnoticed, for it rarely appears alone in its naked state but exists as a substratum of discontent or despair masked by more striking expressions of neurotic illness or by the restless search for feelingfulness. When we think of boredom we are trapped by our preconceived notion of apathy and listlessness—we expect to see someone indolent and inactive, perhaps twitching with impatience, but doing nothing else. We underestimate boredom as its own powerful spur to activity. The chronically bored are often very active people, but they are spurred to action by their urgent quest for feeling. Vigorous activity is ordinarily considered to be the result of strong feeling—people act *because* they feel. The often intense activity of the chronically bored is bound, then, to create a confusing picture unless it can be clearly understood that they act *in an effort* to feel.

The concept of chronic boredom is not meant to be a catchall category, seeking to explain all of human discontent according to one grand plan. It is but one more aspect of the complexity of man's mental function. It seeks not to displace other established categories of psychopathology but to add another dimension of understanding. So the hysterical neurotic or the compulsive neurotic may also harbor the condition of chronic boredom even though the more distressing acute expressions of neuroses may push the manifestations of boredom into the background.

In this chapter I use a case history to illustrate a variety of modes in which chronic boredom may appear. The family described does not exist in actuality, but is a composite formed of unrelated individuals I have studied in varying depths in the course of psychoanalysis, psychotherapy, or a series of diagnostic interviews. To present them as a unified family only facilitates the exposition and does no violence to the fundamental facts. The people are disguised so that they cannot be identified. This literary license is necessary to protect the individuals, but it is also permissible since the purpose of the case history is to illustrate rather than to prove any point in some scientific sense.

THE C. FAMILY

John C., an attractive young man of twenty-one years, dressed casually in jeans and corduroy jacket, claims to be depressed and at loose ends, having no clear idea of what he would like to do with his life. He is presently living at home with his parents after having spent about a year traveling around the country in the vague hope of somehow finding himself through that experience. He had dropped out of a well-known Eastern college early in his sophomore year when he finally realized that he was totally uninterested in what he was doing and had serious questions about the purpose of college.

His travels had taken him first to California to visit his older brother who lives there. Jim, age twenty-four, had also dropped out of college to live for a time in a commune, but he had given that up and now lived with his girl in San Francisco, maintaining a marginal existence by working as a garage mechanic and TV repairman. John stayed with his brother for only a short time, quickly becoming convinced that Jim's life was at least as screwed up as his own and that he was not about to find any helpful answers in the casual and unstructured life that Jim and Jim's friends led. He became uninterested in their drug scenes, their promiscuous sex, and their seemingly endless and aimless talk. He is sympathetic with Jim's view that he must cut himself off completely from their parents to make a life of his own, but he does not share or understand Jim's apparent feeling of bitterness toward their parents, a bitterness that seems to lack specific substance and focus.

John had then wandered up the West Coast, working in mills and on docks, in short-order restaurants and newspaper offices. He toyed with the idea of trying to become a writer but couldn't take himself very seriously; it all seemed so stereotyped and phony. And anyway, he concluded that he really had nothing to say.

He returned to his family home in a wealthy suburb a few months ago, primarily because he was tired of travel and could not think of anything else to do. His parents had accepted his wish to travel on his own for a period of time, hoping that the extended vacation would end with his returning to school with renewed vigor. They had rigorously op-

Chronic Boredom: The Quiet Desperation

posed Jim's decision to drop out and move to a commune in California years earlier, and felt that taking that position had accomplished nothing but the total alienation of their eldest son. This time they determined to try the more accepting approach. But things are wearing pretty thin at home by now, and John wonders how much longer he will be able to continue living there. Although his parents are trying very hard to be accepting and understanding, it is very clear that they are determined that he will return to school, and he is equally determined not to do so. He has been thinking of trying to get a job in the city, has answered some ads and has made a few applications, but he can find nothing that would be of interest to him. He feels guilty about being totally supported by his father and knows that he cannot allow that to continue for long.

John is intellectually superior. His high school academic record was excellent, he had been moderately successful in athletics, and had had an adequate social adjustment throughout his secondary school years, even though he was always a little shy and inhibited with girls. He recalls no particular problems during his childhood, was closer to his mother than to his father, and was always considered to be precociously mature and responsible. High school had been very easy for him for he always knew precisely what was expected of him—he had only to stay out of trouble and keep up with his assignments.

He began to encounter difficulty in the latter half of his first year at college. At first he had done very well, keeping up with his assignments, making friends, and had even considered working on the school newspaper or going out for the track team. But as the year wore on he increasingly found difficulty in concentrating on his academic assignments which seemed to hold no interest for him. He would spend a lot of time just sleeping, watching television, and reading junk magazines and books. Occasional pot parties with friends filled some of the time, but even that failed to be very satisfying. He finished that year with mediocre grades in most of his subjects and an incomplete in one subject where he had failed to complete a number of requirements. He spent a restless summer vacation thereafter, trying to convince himself that he would return to school in the fall and get back on the track. When he did return for his sophomore year, however, things went rapidly downhill. He could not force himself to study, rapidly fell behind, and soon faced the improbable task of catching up. He knew that he would soon have to choose some direction, declare a major, and he felt totally incapable of that selection for he had no notion of which direction he wanted to go in. He had found nothing that interested him.

He acknowledged sex to be something of a problem for him. His first experience with sexual intercourse had been a rather casual affair with a girl he had met during the summer before he started college. He felt clumsy and inhibited with her and, although he was able to consummate the act, was convinced that he was not a very effective lover. He has had sexual intercourse with a number of other girls since that time and feels that he has become less clumsy but probably no more effective, tending always to reach climax too quickly to satisfy his partner. He has been rather disappointed with each sexual experience and believes that sex is greatly overrated. He has little problem in finding girls to date, continues to do so occasionally, but has not found anyone in whom he feels any real interest.

He does smoke pot periodically, preferably when alone and listening to music. It is a source of friction at home, his parents believing pot to have been responsible for his brother's downfall and now the threat of his own. He tries to assure them that it is essentially no different than their use of alcohol, but he cannot seem to make them understand that it is only while smoking that he feels really alive. He has experimented with other drugs in the past but admits that most of it scares him because he has seen a couple of his friends go through some very bad trips.

His attitude toward his parents is a complicated mixture of contempt, good-humored compassion, grudging admiration, and distrust. He says that they now have everything that they've ever wanted: one lovely suburban home, two dogs, three cars, and four children. All that seems to be lacking is happiness.

Mother is described as "flaky"—she's always going to pieces. She goes screaming around the house that her children are driving her crazy, that they're destroying her. "So," he asks, "who told her to have four kids?" On the other hand, he explains that she really is very busy. She is always going to meetings—school activities, political organizations, adult education classes, book clubs—and then there are the luncheons, coffees, and shopping sorties. He wonders if anyone could keep the busy schedule she sets for herself, but he also questions why she has to keep herself so busy. He suspects that she sets that pace to avoid having any time in which to take a good look at her life. And she often drinks a little too much.

His father made it the hard way. He had worked his way through college and law school, with some help from the G.I. Bill. John thinks that his mother also worked as a secretary back in those early days. He doesn't remember his father being home much when he was a youngster. He was always involved in business meetings and worked long hours. Often he would be away on business trips for days at a time. Now he has it made, being the head of a successful business, but he still works sixteen hours a day, six days a week. He comes home from work exhausted, eats dinner, and falls asleep on the couch watching television. John cannot believe that his father really enjoys his work, for he's always complaining about it. When he attempted to talk to his father about cutting down now that things are financially easier, he was brushed aside with some vague answer that if he were to slow down now everything would fall apart, but of course John wouldn't understand how those things work. He admires his father's endurance and determination, but he wonders what it's all for, since father never seems to have any time in which to enjoy all of the things that he has worked so hard to acquire. And he often drinks too much.

He sees his parents' relationship to be empty. They never have very much to say to each other and they rarely do things together except to go out on Saturday night and Sunday to drink with friends who also drink a lot. They never take vacations. Mother often nags father to take time off to go on one trip or another, but he always seems to have a million reasons to explain that this is the very worst time to think of leaving the business unattended.

John thinks that they have probably been very good parents. They have never neglected the children and, in fact, always seem to consider the children first. They have never been excessively strict or demanding; they have actually been very permissive and understanding. Yet John admits that he feels as Jim does, that to live his own life he must somehow be able to completely break with his parents. He feels that he is a disappointment to them, and so are the rest of the kids in the family. He feels guilty about that and wishes that he could manage to be more of what they expect him to be, but to do that he would have to live his life as they have lived theirs, and he finds that impossible to contemplate.

John describes his sister Susie, age eighteen, as a total mess. She is constantly overweight, constantly depressed, and in everlasting battle with mother. Always a mediocre student, never very popular with her own age group, she seems to hate everyone and everything in the world, including herself. She has barely managed to get through high school, refuses to go to college, and is presently in a running battle with both parents about her desire to move into her own apartment. She claims to be in love with a twenty-six-year-old ex-ministry student whom their parents describe as a professional demonstrator for abstruse causes, a proponent of transcendental meditation, a leader of sensitivity training groups, and a bum without any visible means of support. John feels sorry for Susie and wishes that she could really be in love with this

Chronic Boredom: The Quiet Desperation

fellow, but feels that her demands and assertions are meant primarily to get a response from her parents. He believes that all of her harangues about sexual freedom are pure bluff and that she'd be scared to death if she ever found herself in bed with a man. He has tried to get closer to Susie these past few months, feeling that she really needs help from someone, but Susie resents and distrusts him almost as much as she distrusts their parents.

Charlie is only fifteen, and he may be in the worst trouble of all. John chuckles whimsically as he describes Charlie's spirited rebelliousness—cutting classes, running with the pack who are already well into marijuana, hard liquor, and gambling, his arrogant dismissal of all parental limitations, and his few brushes with the local law concerning episodes that at least bordered on the delinquent. Charlie is really very bright, but he may never even get as far as finishing high school. He is an excellent athlete, and John hopes that athletics may be Charlie's salvation. Recently some of the coaches have talked to him about taking team sports more seriously, and Charlie is just interested enough in that sort of thing to buckle down and stick with school to be able to play on some of the teams. But if he does stick with school, that will be the only reason, for Charlie is already quite convinced that all of that book learning is only for suckers and squares, and he flatly states that he does not intend to be one of the meek sitting around waiting to inherit the earth.

John views his family, including himself, as a tragic example of something that has gone wrong for a lot of people, the victims of some indefinable malfunction of an imcomprehensible world. He sometimes thinks about suicide, but even as he thinks about it he knows that he would not actually go through with it. Things would have to get worse. He has fantasies of being a traveling musician or an itinerant newspaper reporter, moving on as whim moves him. He feels out of joint with the world, not knowing where he fits or what this life is supposed to be all about. He longs to find something that he feels is really important, but whatever that might be, he has not found it yet.

John's father, Donald C., is not quite as tall as John, but he is more massively built. A serious and intense man in his early fifties, he is a little overweight and puffy-eyed, assertive in manner, soft-spoken but direct in his speech. He is perplexed, hurt, and angry, for he feels that his world has gone awry and he is unable to understand the reason. He states that he has worked hard all of his life to provide his family with those things that seemed to him to be desirable, and he feels that he has been more than moderately successful. Despite that success, his family is a shambles. His wife is unhappy, always complaining, always wanting something more. His two oldest sons have dropped out of college—Jim, living with some dumb broad in California, willing to settle for the life of a grease monkey; John, a lazy drifter waiting for life to be handed to him on a platter. When he speaks of Susie, an expression of disgust flashes briefly. She's been on one kind of diet or another as far back as he can remember, she's sloppy, a real pseudointellectual, always blabbing about women's rights and capitalistic materialism. He thinks she's really so dumb that she's trying hard to become a hippie without even realizing that she's years too late to hop onto that old bandwagon. Despite his harsh words, one has the feeling that he is most hurt and disappointed by her. About Charlie he is still optimistic. "Oh, he gets himself into all kinds of minor trouble and he's not doing very well with his studies, but at least he's alive, a real go-getter. He's just going through that phase that all kids go through. He'll grow out of it and be okay."

He clearly feels overburned and emotionally undernourished. His protest that he continues to work so hard out of financial necessity is easily overcome, and he realizes that the only reason that he spends so much time at work now, is that it is the only thing with which he feels comfortable. It gives some form and purpose to his life. When he does spend

Chronic Boredom: The Quiet Desperation

more time at home, his wife is constantly at him to do something about the children, to straighten them out. "You're their father," he mimics, "you're supposed to know how to make them shape up!" He shrugs, disheartened, admitting that he really doesn't know what more to do about them. He feels he's cared for them, provided them with the means to become any worthwhile thing they'd like to be, but beyond that he doesn't know how to make them grow up, how to make them want to be worthwhile adults.

He has been truly surprised by the gradually dawning awareness that he and his wife are strangers to each other. He is certain that once they were really close, back in those busy days when the kids were coming and they were working hard to build a life for their family. He reminisces briefly about some of the good times they had then, but now his wife seems to be totally dissatisfied with him. She wants him to be intellectual, artistic, romantic, and all sorts of things that he feels that he is not and never was. He claims to respect her for all that she has accomplished, but thinks that she has no real understanding or appreciation of him.

He's had his share of extramarital affairs over the years. None of them was serious, but occasionally he has felt some wish for novelty. His sexual relationship with his wife has been okay, but it's been a long, long time since there was any real excitement in it. A secret affair, whatever drawbacks it might have, still has the excitement of the chase about it, the planning and arranging that lends some eager anticipation to the whole thing. He believes that his wife is not a very sensual person. He has often had the impression that if she never had any more sex she'd not even miss it.

At home he maintains a steady position—hard work, responsibility, loyalty, the family—these are the values that are worthwhile. But he admits that there are times when he secretly wishes that he could duck out, just throw the whole thing up for grabs and start all over, free and clear. Perhaps he married too soon, boxed himself in to family responsibility too early, passing up the opportunity to be free to discover what he really wanted to do with his life. As he muses these thoughts he smiles wryly, suddenly aware that he is saying things now that sound very much like the things his son, John, has said to him. This is part of his perplexity, for he knows that he admires John in some way for the position he has taken about his own life, yet his sense of fatherly responsibility demands of him that he oppose his son on many of those issues with which he secretly agrees. But then, almost shaking himself back to reality, he firmly reasserts his view that one must sacrifice dreams of happiness for the hard-headed obligations of life. And behind that firm assertion there is the hint of a plea for support, for some affirmation of the validity of his position.

Andrea C., John's mother, is a slender, attractive woman in her late forties who appears to be always in motion, even while sitting. She is disappointed. Life has not turned out to be what she had expected. Perhaps her mistake was her failure to continue her own education, to have developed a profession that would have provided her with some feeling of doing something of consequence.

She was young when she married. Donald had just come out of the army and had returned to the university to continue his education. She had worked as a secretary, as a part-time waitress, at any job she could find, and with his army benefits they were able to make it. Everyone seemed to be in a great big hurry back in those days, she recalls, because of the years lost in the war, the uncertainty of the school years that followed, and the intense feeling of competition that pervaded their world then. They all felt that they were behind schedule. They had their family very quickly—four kids in nine years—and that was a very busy time. Donald got his law degree and went to work for a business concern. It was a very demanding job, involving long hours and frequent business trips, but he had worked hard and had been very successful. She was often lonely then, but she had a number of good friends from the university years who were much in the same boat, and they all helped each other out. The children were young and needed her; her life was filled with their busy schedules, and she was constantly delighted by their development and growth. In raising her children she felt that she was doing something important.

Suddenly tearful, she questions what she did wrong. She believes that she did everything that she could to make her children's lives secure and meaningful and rich. The constant trips to museums and playgrounds once they were old enough to walk; the careful selection of nursery schools even though, in the beginning, that had added to their financial burden. And now that the children are older, they all seem to be so unhappy, so lost. Nothing seems to have any meaning to any of them. And then, just as suddenly, she is angry and accuses this crazy mixed-up world of being at fault. Crooked politicians, senseless wars, massive poverty and starvation, the ever-present threat of nuclear annihilation— how could anyone grow up in such a world with a belief in anything?

Then Donald receives his share of her anger. He got so caught up in his success that he never really spent enough time with the children; kids need to spend time with their fathers if they're to learn the real values in life. He is also anything but a young maiden's dream of what a husband should be. She feels that he has been very inattentive to her for a long time. He works so long and hard that he has no energy left for anything when he comes home. He has no interest in her activities and she has become increasingly aware of the fact that they have very little to talk about.

She spends her days in various organizational activities, tries to continue her own education, manages the home, but still she feels she is doing nothing consequential. She feels that she is a totally unimportant person because she is doing nothing important.

For some time she has been having a secret sexual affair with the husband of a friend. Their clandestine meetings are crowded into the midst of her busy afternoons. It is not a wholly satisfying arrangement—she hates the secrecy and deceit—but it gives her some little feeling that she is appreciated by someone. He is an intelligent man, sensitive and artistic—all of the things that her husband is not. This is not her first affair, but she feels justified in seeking her own sexual satisfaction since her husband seems to have completely forgotten that she is a woman.

The C. family present a varied picture of discontent. They are an unhappy lot, but what portion of their unhappiness can be ascribed to chronic boredom? Perhaps they portray nothing more than the expectable dissatisfactions with life, an expression of the "human condition," even in slightly exaggerated form. Acceptance of that position would be nothing more than resignation to a malignant fate that mysteriously determines man's lot to be filled with woe. We may be forced ultimately to accept that dismal imperative, but we should not prematurely foreclose on the possibility of achieving happiness lest, by doing so, we needlessly guarantee the continuance of discontent.

When we see unhappiness in the lives of the unfortunate poor, sick, and oppressed, we are touched by it and we understand its source. The C. family does not fit that picture, for they live a realized dream. Health and wealth are theirs, wholesome surroundings, education—all that should be required for the free pursuit of happiness. We do not need their example to prove to us once more that happiness is not merely the sum of our externalities, no matter how fortunate. Internal conflicts may plague the fortunate as well as the unfortunate. Depression does not afflict only the poor and anxiety is not restricted to the socially oppressed. Anxiety and depression are manifestly present in the members of the C. family, and chronic boredom is there as well.

OTHER SYMPTOMS OBSCURE BOREDOM

Suzie C. is not unaware of her boredom. Her obesity is only moderate, but a constant source of distress for her, and she makes the interesting observation that she eats too much because everything is so boring. School is boring, her friends are boring, her family is boring . . . "the whole world is blah!" Only when she feels that she is in love does she lose the desire to overeat, and then she loses weight quite without effort. One quickly sees an obvious connection; she substitutes food for the love that she longs for. But she corrects that misimpression. It is loving that makes the difference, not being loved. She recalls a number of instances when she felt "madly in love" with one young man or another who did not reciprocate her feelings, and her anguish at those times was great, but life then was not boring. On the other hand, being loved by someone that she did not love did nothing for her boredom or for her overeating.

She is not afraid of sex, as John supposed. She considers herself to be a veteran in sexual matters, having had sexual intercourse with a number of young men over the course of the last two or more years. She finds sex to be pleasant enough, even though she has not experienced orgasm. It is the physical contact, the touching and embracing, that pleases her, and the comfortable informality of lying in bed with someone. She wishes that she could experience orgasm but shrugs it off, believing that her hang-up will disappear with time and more experience.

There is about Suzie a distinct impression of immaturity, of childishness, but that alone cannot explain the specific manifestations of her unhappiness. That she constantly seeks stimulation through oral indulgence and bodily contact attests to her immaturity, but her constant search for stimulation points to her chronic boredom. The two are not mutually exclusive; immaturity and chronic boredom are often found together.

Charlie C. could be easily dismissed as a troublesome adolescent, but that might be a serious error. The popular view of adolescence as a turbulent phase of development is well founded, and that makes the recognition of psychopathology during that period all the more difficult. All kinds of variant behavior may be attributed to adolescence and thereby shrugged off with the optimistic expectation that time alone will calm the troubled waters. Time is important for the resolution of adolescent problems, but not all problems in the adolescent are to be attributed to adolescence itself.

Charlie's defiance of authority is extreme, pushing, at times transgressing, the limits of legality. Perhaps more matter for concern than his encounters with the law are the frequent exposures of himself to danger that must violate the limits of his own common sense. Yet he is far from stupid and claims to be quite aware of what he is doing. It is all a part of his life scheme, consciously expressed, for he is determined to avoid the deadness and dullness that characterizes the lives of the adults he sees around him.

The entire C. family is bored, but he claims that he is not, for he dedicates himself to the pursuit of excitement. An avowed thrill seeker at the age of fifteen! How strenuously he must defend himself against the lurking boredom just beneath his self-created surface turbulence. Like a young Nietzsche, he has rediscovered his master's admonition, " . . the secret of the greatest fruitfulness and the greatest enjoyment of existence is: To live dangerously! Build your cities under Veruvius. Send your ships into unchartered seas. . . ." Danger does evoke the excitement of fear, creating the sense of liveliness, but to what lengths will he be forced in his effort to maintain that level of intensity? What eventual risks will be required to stir him up? Adolescent he is, but he is responding to a deeper, more pervasive problem of chronic boredom.

My intention here is not to dismiss the effects of immaturity or of adolescence as unimportant only then to explain their manifestations on the alternative basis of chronic boredom. It is, instead, to demonstrate that chronic boredom may coexist with a variety of other states and conditions that can mask or obscure its own impelling effects.

Chronic boredom is the expression of successful and extensive repression of feelings. Since all neurotic psychopathology may be viewed as a result of an effort to avoid feelings that are unpleasurable or that seem dangerous, one begins to see the complex relationship between chronic boredom and the usually recognized forms of neurotic psychopathology like hysteria and obsessive-compulsive neurosis. To the extent that any neurotic adaptation entails extensive repression of feelings, chronic boredom is also involved. Sometimes chronic boredom with its typical manifestations of restlessness and apathy, disinterest, emptiness, and loneliness is, itself, the central picture of the presenting pathology. Often it is present and involved, but obscured by the more dramatic symptoms of the neurosis.

CHRONIC BOREDOM AND CHARACTER

Wilhelm Reich (1930) suggested that the neuroses arise as emergency measures to fill a breach in the character structures of individuals. This provides a starting point from which we may view the relationship between character, character neurosis, symptom neurosis, and chronic boredom.

Character or character structure is not in and of itself pathological but is an adaptive structure that develops in the interaction between the individual's inherited constitution and his experience. It is the unique organization of values, attitudes, and modes of action and reaction that is typical of an individual. When someone expresses a view or behaves in some way that is not typical of that person, we say that "that is not like him" or that he is acting "out of character." One central aspect of character is the typical way the individual deals with his feelings. One person tends always toward intensity in experiencing and expressing feelings, while another tends always to be reserved and cool. Or a specific feeling or constellation of feelings may be dominant in different individuals, so that one may be joyful, another angry and disgruntled, a third sad and pessimistic, and so on.

There is wide variation in feeling intensity in different individuals from the start, ranging from those infants who are highly reactive to those that tend to be relatively placid, and those differences we must attribute to constitutional make-up. Beyond that, however, what gives to each developing character its unique stamp of feeling coloration is the individual's life experiences. As the individual's experience gives rise predominantly to pleasurable and comfortable feelings, so he will tend to continue to be open to his feelings, and his evolving personality will be marked by that openness. But as his experience gives rise mainly to painful or unpleasurable feelings, and feelings that he comes to perceive as dangerous, then he may have to defend himself against those feelings. The defenses employed exact a toll, becoming a part of the character structure of that individual and placing some constraint upon his evolving personality. As the requirement for such defensive operations is greater, the more will the evolving character be deformed by the incorporation of those defenses.

There is no sharp or clear line of demarcation between character and character neurosis. That distinction is a matter of judgment based upon the cost to the individual of the defensive deformation of his character structure. The incorporated defenses will be apparent in a particular character structure, but as long as that person is able to love and to work effectively, his character will be considered normal. Only when the defensive deformation of character is sufficient to seriously impede that person's ability to love and to work effectively will that be judged a character neurosis. One person employing typical obsessive-compulsive defenses may be characteristically neat, orderly, careful, constrained, and have a tendency toward intellectualization. His would be termed a compulsive character structure but would fall within the normal range so long as those defensive manifestations did not interfere with his capacity for work and his ability to love. Another person, employing the same set of defenses but whose defensive need for order is so great that he finds himself spending hours each day making lists of things to do instead of being productive, will be adjudged to have a character neurosis. And so will he whose intellectualizing defenses are so strong that he allows himself no awareness of feelings for others, and whose constraint and need for control interferes with close and intimate relationships. Everyone's character is marked to some degree by the psychic defenses he has incorporated in his adaptive structure. It is a matter of judgment when those incorporated defenses sufficiently deform that structure so that it becomes maladaptive rather than adaptive.

In character structure and in character neurosis the manifestations of defensive deformation tend to be "ego-syntonic"—that is, they seem to be reasonable, even valuable, ways to be to the person himself. In the symptom neuroses that is not so. The manifestations of the symptom neuroses, hysteria and obsessive-compulsive neurosis, are much more circumscribed and tend to be "ego-dystonic,"—they appear to the individual to be alien intrusions having no logical explanation or social value. Whereas the person with a compulsive character neurosis sees his neatness and orderliness as the correct way to be, he who has an obsessive-compulsive neurosis views his hand-washing compulsion or his obsessive doubting about everything as a symptom. It is behavior that intrudes upon him despite his will to do otherwise. It has no apparent meaning or social value, and creates only distress. In Wilhelm Reich's view, the symptom neuroses arise as an emergency defense when the ordinary character defenses of an individual fail. Thus, it is usual to find that the person with an obsessive-compulsive neurosis has an underlying compulsive character structure, the hysteric an underlying hysterical character structure.

The human mind has available a wide variety of defensive mechanisms to protect against the conscious awareness of feelings that are deemed unacceptable or dangerous. All of the defensive mechanisms have that ultimate objective, and which mechanisms are preferred by an individual is determined by his constitution and his experience.

As we have seen, the primary mechanism of defense for everyone is repression, the process of blocking thoughts and feelings from entering conscious awareness. All other mechanisms of defense may be considered as secondary processes that function to support and reinforce the primary mechanism of repression. Because the feelings are not annihilated by repression, they are constantly present in the unconscious and are pressing toward conscious awareness. Repression, to be effective, must be an equally constant effort. The secondary mechanisms of defense serve to reinforce or to lighten the required effort.

Thoughts and feelings are tightly connected in the human mind, so the secondary mechanism of splitting the thought from the feeling lightens the effort of repression required, since now only the thought *or* the feeling has to be repressed. For example, anyone would expect that the thought, "I'd like to punch him in the nose," would be accompanied by an angry feeling. However, the thought can be split off from the angry feeling, and then either the thought or the feeling may be repressed. I believe this split is where we find the distinction between obsessive-compulsive defenses and hysterical defenses. The obsessive-compulsive represses the feeling and then is obsessed with the idea of punching noses, but feels no anger that would prompt him to act on the idea. The hysteric, on the other hand, represses the idea but not the anger, so he is often angry but doesn't know with whom he is angry nor why. The compulsive is then seen to be intellectualizing and affectively flat, while the hysteric is seen to be emotionally labile but inappropriately so, and has ideational blindspots.

Chronic boredom is the consequence of repression of feelings built into the character structure of the individual and is therefore to be considered a character neurosis. It is probably the basic character neurosis, just as repression is the primary mechanism of defense. The secondary mechanisms of defense, however, often come into play to support the repressive effort and obscure the "pure" picture of boredom by superimposing the effects of obsessive-compulsive or hysterical defenses.

In the C. family, described above, John comes closest to portraying the undistorted picture of chronic boredom. His father, Donald, presents the picture of chronic boredom partially obscured by his obsessive-compulsive defenses, and Andrea's chronic boredom is obscured mostly by her hysterical defenses. Susie employs both hysterical and compulsive defenses, but is quite aware of her constant feeling of boredom. As for Charlie, perhaps it is too early to draw final conclusions, but his search for thrills leads him to behavior that at least looks like that of the psychopathic or sociopathic personality. And all of them manifest depression of various degrees—not depression of the melancholic variety, but the specific depression of chronic boredom.

THE DEPRESSION OF CHRONIC BOREDOM

When Andrea C. first appeared seeking help, there was no suggestion of boredom in the picture that she presented. She was a mass of tortured anxiety that had seized her quite suddenly and recently. She was constantly fearful of impending catastrophe. She became convinced that she had left the gas stove burning or that some appliance would overheat and start a fire whenever she left her home. Height scared her, open spaces created a vague but penetrating dread. She avoided elevators whenever she could walk stairs instead. She feared that she was going crazy and wondered about the advisability of hospitalization.

The intensity of her anxiety subsided remarkably in the

course of several diagnostic interviews and she felt greatly relieved. Psychoanalytic treatment was initiated and it was quickly apparent that the sudden dissipation of much of her anxiety was due to no internal change but to some sense of assurance that everything would now be under control. And, indeed, she became very controlled. Filled with gratitude for the relief that she felt, she praised the analyst and the treatment for the wonders that had been wrought. Even the lower level of anxiety that had persisted seemed to evaporate and soon she talked of "feeling her old self" once again. And then the praise gradually gave way to grumbling discontent. Life seemed now to be dull and pointless. She claimed to find no reason now to get out of bed for each day seemed like any other, unremarkable and without purpose. This was "her old self," now returned, for she could easily recognize and identify this present state of feeling with the feelings that she had had for a long time before the onset of her anxiety. She despaired of finding pleasure, satisfaction, enjoyment—those were concepts now far removed. She complained bitterly of the analyst and the analysis, holding them responsible for her present "deadness." She even longed for a return of her anxiety; then, at least, she had felt alive. She spoke of suicide, insistently reiterating her view that the world was no damned good and that life wasn't worth living.

Her former state of anxiety had dissipated, to be replaced by a state of depression that had long preexisted her episode of anxiety. Now the underlying depression was clearly exposed and readily identified. Why, then, complicate matters further by suggesting that she suffers from chronic boredom? Is not depression sufficiently complex and difficult to treat without the introduction of new complications?

Difficult and complex it is, but that is precisely the point. Were depression a simple, straightforward matter with a clearly defined set of manifestations and an equally clear explication of its process and course, there would be no reason to look further. But that is far from the present state of our knowledge. What is called depression appears to be a group of disorders sharing the common symptom of a depressive mood but otherwise manifesting a range of symptoms and having a variety of causes.

Compare, for example, that form of depression sometimes called melancholia with the particular picture of depression presented by Andrea. The melancholic appears always to hate himself. He loudly proclaims his worthlessness, his evilness, and clearly states his conviction that he does not deserve to live. Andrea—like many who share her form of depression— claimed instead that the *world* is no good and that life isn't *worth* living. Now these are very different expressed attitudes, but are they reflective of some basic difference in two forms of depression or are they merely varied expressions of the same or similar underlying pathology?

When we consider the generally agreed upon mechanism of melancholia, we have to recognize that these differing expressions must relate to two quite separate pathological processes. The melancholic, unable to express his rage toward the outside world for fear of losing those upon whom he desperately depends, is forced therefore to turn his rage back upon himself and so hates himself. Andrea, although depressed, has no difficulty in expressing her anger, her rage, toward the external world. She does not question her right to live but rather doubts that living is worth her while. The mechanism of rage turned back upon the self is not operative in Andrea, so her depression cannot be explained on the same basis as in melancholia.

Andrea presents a picture, widespread, of the specific depression of chronic boredom. It is the expression of a sense of hopelessness, of despair of ever being able to experience the liveliness necessary for joy and happiness, or even peaceful comfort.

Donald's compulsive character structure contrasts sharply with Andrea's hysterical character, yet the depressive mood that brought him finally into treatment was remarkably like Andrea's in every detail. He, too, showed little evidence of self-hatred but found his world to be disappointing in all respects. Despite his accumulated wealth and all that it could buy, he found little joy or pleasure in his life and seriously questioned the value of living. He had worked hard and long, had been led by good intentions, and now he believed that there had to be something more to life than he had found.

His analysis was marked at the outset with a dull dreariness. Flat in tone, repetitive in content, he despaired of finding purpose or meaning in his life. He came, in time, to be aware of his own flat reportorial tone, his preoccupation with repetitive detail, and he felt certain that the analyst must be profoundly bored by him. The suggestion that he, the patient, must be feeling very bored struck a responsive chord, and he admitted that he was, indeed, bored to death. He began to understand that his boredom was the consequence of his extensive repression of all feelings that he believed to be unacceptable, and we began to explore some of those feelings. Now he became increasingly restive and dissatisfied, and a tinge of angry discontent colored his tone.

At this time it became necessary for him to make a short business trip, and when he returned he reported a new experience. He had developed a fear of flying. Dimly aware of some uneasiness upon boarding the plane, he later was seized by an intense fear of crashing when his plane encountered some mild turbulence in flight. Shaken by the experience, he vowed that he would cancel his return flight and return by train. Nevertheless, he did return by plane and again experienced anxiety, although this time with lesser intensity. Then he developed some sense of pressure in his chest and became convinced that he was having, or was about to have, a heart attack. Repeated examinations and reassurances by his trusted family physician did little to relieve his anxiety. His flat, dull, controlled manner had changed. Now he was restless, impatient, constantly anxious, and he complained bitterly that it was the analysis that had brought this unwanted change. He wished now only to be relieved of his uncomfortable anxiety and return to the former "comfort" of his life.

As was the case with Andrea, Donald's anxiety subsided

and disappeared in time, to be replaced by the earlier flat, controlled, monotonous state that was far more familiar to him. And as it had been with Andrea, Donald at first welcomed the return of "his old self" with profound relief, only then to grow increasingly discontented with the dullness and emptiness of his life. He, too, then expressed regret that his anxiety now was gone for, uncomfortable as that anxiety had been, at least he had had a hopeful expectation that something was happening, that something within him was changing. Now he felt hopeless once again, convinced that neither analysis nor anything else could relieve him of the dullness of his unfeeling life.

CYCLES OF ANXIETY AND BOREDOM

Donald's anxiety did return in time, as did Andrea's. This repetitive pattern tends to be typical in the analyses of the chronically bored—recurring cycles of boredom and anxiety, each phase replacing the other and each phase experienced as intolerable discomfort for its own reasons. But with each repeated cycle some analytic work is accomplished, freeing up the individual's capacity to be aware of feelings and reducing his attendant anxiety about being more intensely feelingful.

This cyclical pattern emerged clearly in John's analysis, as well. Starting off in a moderately depressed, low-keyed mood, he too despaired of finding meaningfulness in his life. If only he could find something that seemed to him to be important! In some abstract sense he could agree that there were many things in his life's experience that might be adjudged important from an objective point of view, but that mattered little. Nothing *felt* important to him. He had tried to throw himself wholeheartedly into many things, sometimes with brief success at the outset, but even then running out of steam in a very short time. He would lose interest and become again depressed and dissatisfied.

As his analysis proceeded John experienced the swing from boredom to mild anxiety and back several times, and some increased capacity for feeling became evident in the importance he was coming to attach to his analysis and to his relationship to the analyst. Now he looked forward to his sessions and was aware of missing them when interruptions intervened. He felt some hopeful anticipation that things could get better.

Fear of Feelings

At this time John met a young woman who interested him and his excitement *and* his anxiety became intense. He longed to be with her, yet he dreaded every meeting. When with her he would become tongue-tied, feel awkward and clumsy, wish only to escape. He believed that she would see him as an immature schoolboy and, despite her obvious interest in him, he was convinced that if she really came to know him she'd feel no interest at all.

This was a marked departure from his past behavior with women. He had always been aloof and disdainful, unruffled and unimpressed. Now he had lost his cool when he most wanted to appear to be impressively strong, confident, and sophisticated. His anxiety was tied directly to his excitement, and this interlude enabled John to recognize and to distinguish those two feelings and their relationship to each other. It was the feeling of excitement, pleasurable in itself, that aroused his uncomfortable anxiety. That became graphically clear to him one evening at a party where everyone was a little bit high. A girl he had known for many years confided to him in a giggled whisper that she was so excited by something going on at the party that she was afraid that she might wet her pants, and he suddenly saw himself reflected in that off-hand remark.

He was not certain that his anxiety was that specific, that he feared wetting his pants, but he did then recall a time in nursery school at age three when he had done so, and all the kids had laughed at him. His humiliation had been most painful. Now he recognized his fear that, under the pressure of feelings that stirred him in the presence of his new girlfriend, he would "lose control," behave in some way that would reveal him to be clumsy and immature. The pants-wetting episode in nursery school was not a root cause of his anxiety but the recollection of this episode did enable John to crystalize in his own mind a pattern of fear of humiliation that had haunted him throughout his life. John now recognized that he was constantly on guard against revealing anything about himself that might possibly be considered childish and therefore shameful.

The fact that John's sexual and loving feelings were not the exclusive focus at this time was clear, for angry and competitive feelings were also entering his awareness with greater intensity than before—and with very much the same effects. He recognized that he was now playing tennis differently, for example. He felt a strong desire to win, was hitting cleaner and harder shots, but he also felt that same trembling fear when in a closely contested match. He would usually lose those matches because of his tendency, then, to tighten up, to overcontrol his swing. His fear was that his competitive excitement, his wish to "blast his opponent off the court," would result in erratic and clumsy play.

These developments in John's analysis can help us to understand the basis for the to-and-fro pattern between anxiety and boredom that is so often encountered in the analysis of the chronically bored. The recurring cycles of anxiety and boredom reflect the conflict between the wish to experience strong feelings and the fear of the consequence of doing so. Within the safety of the analytic situation feelings begin to approach the patient's conscious awareness with increasing strength, but as they do, there is also growing anxiety about his or her ability to handle these feelings in appropriate ways. As the anxiety becomes too intense it triggers the old repressive defense against feelings and boredom returns once more. Each repetition of the cycle, however, allows the patient to gain greater familiarity with his or her feelings so the anxiety about them gradually diminishes.

At this stage in his analysis John was not predominately concerned with oedipal conflicts. Taboo incestuous wishes, guilt over murderous rivalries with brothers and father—those would emerge later. For now the conflicts centered mainly around issues of self-regulation, self-control, when under the pressure of intense feelings. In the past John had consistently received his parents' implicit and explicit message that strong feelings as well as the behaviors prompted by those feelings were unacceptable. In response to this message John had established a mechanism for maintaining self-control by repressing the intensity of his feelings, but that had deprived him of the pleasurable experience of excitement and interest. It had created his characterological condition of chronic boredom. Now, if John was to allow himself the newfound pleasure of liveliness, he would have to develop a whole new mechanism for the adequate regulation of his feeling tensions. That would involve a totally new orientation for him, one that required a clear distinction between the experience of feelings and the expression of feelings. He had to learn that he could tolerate the tension of a strong feeling while delaying discharge in behavior, allowing his judgment to intervene and determine appropriate modes of behavior.

Analysis reveals that the initial central concern of the chronically bored is always the fear that they will be shamed and humiliated by the revelation of their inability to handle themselves effectively under the pressure of intense feelings. Often this anxiety is not their only problem, for they may also have the full range of oedipal conflicts, guilt, and castration anxiety that we have come to recognize as important in the various psychoneuroses and character disorders. Those who have early learned to regulate their tension and to control their behavior by massively repressing intense feelings, however, find themselves readily able to defend against the anxieties of oedipal conflicts by repressing those feelings, too. Then the oedipal significance of their feelings will be unappreciated and interpretations at that level will be no more than intellectual exercise. The chronically bored must first be helped to find the courage to experience their feelings with full awareness and only then will the specific conflictual significance of their feelings become understandable and resolvable.

THE SEARCH FOR FEELINGS

The fear of the chronically bored that they will be overwhelmed by feelings, will be pushed by feelings to inappropriate or humiliating behavior, is constantly countered by their restless craving to be feelingful and lively. So Susie C. engages in promiscuous sexual activity not because she is driven to that by strong sexual feelings but because she hopes that sexual activity will enable her to feel something. In sexual activity she does feel something, she experiences sensation. Her overeating is a similar sensory event. Sensation is not feeling, but it is experiential, and for many of those blocked from feeling awareness, sensory awareness becomes the best available substitute. Food, sex, and drugs are the principal avenues in this restless pursuit of sensation, often to the serious detriment of the sensation seeker. Yet the motive is not self-destruction, nor is it some masochistic enjoyment of pain and suffering. Those unhappy consequences are only the unsought byproducts of the imperative quest for sensation as substitute for blocked feelings.

As we have seen, the customary assumption that vigorous activity is motivated by strong and appropriate feelings is often in error. Sexual activity is not always the expression of sexual feelings, eating is not always the expression of feelings of hunger. As Susie pursues her sexual encounters for the pleasurable sensory stimulation that they provide, so Andrea engages in extramarital sex for a variety of motives that have little or nothing to do with sexual feelings. Mainly it is the thrill of participating in something illicit, the excitement of running a risk. When she meets her secret lover she experiences a heightened awareness of herself, a sense of being naughty. After each secret meeting her mind is filled with concerns about being discovered. She wonders if she was seen, if someone suspects, if her lover will tell. She fears that she, herself, will accidentally slip and reveal the truth. On the surface it appears to be inexplicable behavior. Does she wish to punish herself to alleviate some deep sense of guilt? Does she simply enjoy creating this burden of fear and dread? Were the sexual episodes truly gratifying we might understand the trade-off—pleasurable sex outweighing the inconvenience and the painful fear. But her own admission reveals that her illicit affairs are no more sexually gratifying than is sex with her own husband.

In the course of her analysis it was possible to observe this behavior closely, for she was involved in one of her extramarital affairs. In time she was able to recognize that this affair, like the previous ones, followed a particular pattern. At first there had been the hopeful anticipation, the sense of naughtiness, the exciting fear of being found out. Then, as the newness wore off, there came a feeling of disappointment, of being let down, and a restless dissatisfaction with the tawdriness and inconvenience of their arrangement. As the dissatisfaction mounted, so did the preoccupation with concerns of being discovered. Yet, paradoxically, she took ever greater risks as her fear of discovery rose. She began to insist upon meeting her lover in public places, even to the point of attending a play with him one evening when her husband was working late.

She was amazed by the discovery of her own wish to be caught by her husband. That which she had dreaded so was also her own undeniable wish. She puzzled over this discovery. She had no desire for divorce, that would only leave her even more alone. She wondered what would really happen if Donald found out, and she laughed gaily as she pictured his

Chronic Boredom: The Quiet Desperation

indignant wrath. "Boy! Would that ever be a fight!" And then she remembered the fights that they used to have and, surprisingly, that was a fond memory.

She and Donald had not had those fights in recent years, but there was a period in their marriage—a long period—when they had had frequent and furious battles. Not at the beginning of their marriage; they had both been far too busy then. It started after five or six years of marriage had passed, when things were getting a bit easier for them. She couldn't clearly recall the causes of those furious battles but assumed that they were the usual things that married people fight over—spending money, how to raise the children, paying more attention to each other. Those fights, furious and frenzied, had always ended happily in sexual reconciliation, and afterward they would laugh as they tried to figure out what the fight had really been about.

Now she wanted another fight with Donald, not to hurt him or herself, but to recreate the scene for another of those delightful reconciliations. No longer could they fight over money, for that would be silly. They couldn't fight about raising children who were already grown. The only reasonable issue would be infidelity. And in this way Andrea became aware of what she termed "the joys of marital strife!" How far far better to fight, to scream, to cry, to despair, and then make love, than to endure forever this empty, unfeeling life together. Anything to stir the passions, to get the juices flowing once again.

Donald had no fear of being discovered in his sexual escapades outside of marriage, for he took great care in maintaining secrecy. His affairs were brief, usually one-nighters, and never involved a woman that had any connection with his own social set or business relations. He preferred tougher stock, women who were depreciated in his view, women whom he called "sexual technicians." Sometimes professional whores, sometimes not, they were all characterized as tough, experienced women who knew all the tricks. With them he felt able to take off all restraints, to be as aggressive, as ruthless, as experimental as he wished to be. There was clearly little of love in those sexual exchanges, even though the external form was that of love. He was sure that if he caused these women pain, they loved it, and if he demeaned them, it only stirred their passions to greater heights. Beyond that, he rarely saw the women again, so why care what they might think of him!

Under those circumstances he became a vigorous and passionate sexual participant, far more alive and energetic than ever he found himself to be when in bed with his own wife. With Andrea, he felt constrained to be tender and gentle, considerate of her sensitivities, respectful of her delicacy. Convinced of her conventionality, he was certain that she would be disgusted by his wish to experiment, to engage in perverse activities, to be aggressively assertive. What would she think of him if he behaved so with her?! Donald was quite certain that no "decent" woman would tolerate such behavior, that she would forever after see her husband as a depraved, revolting, animalistic boor. He had some reason on his side, for Andrea did have her interfering inhibitions. What he failed to realize was her underlying wish for help in breaking through them.

Nonetheless, Donald's attitudes had familiar antecedents long predating his relationship with Andrea. Those attitudes had their roots in the often-found splitting of the child's image of the mother into a "good" mother and a "bad" mother—the one characterized as respected and idealized (asexual) and the other depreciated and feared (sexual). This mental device, particularly common in the compulsive character organization, facilitates the repression of the child's forbidden sexual wishes toward the mother, and leads to the subsequent common adolescent distinction between "good girls" (asexual) and "bad girls" (sexual).

In all of this description there is nothing that will strike the experienced psychologist as novel or unfamiliar. It is a well-known picture. But what does it reveal of Donald's feelings in reference to his active sexual behavior with his depreciated "one-night stands"? As he describes those episodes, one is impressed by the absence of loving feelings; one sees evidence only of aggression and anger. With Andrea he tends toward gentleness, passivity, and a lack of sexuality. Are we to assume, then, that his sexuality is fundamentally and historically tied to feelings of aggression and anger, not love?

Donald himself is aware of a certain patterned response. After an episode of "vulgar sexual discharge" with some depreciated women, he finds himself more actively interested in, and affectionate toward, his own wife for a variable period of time. Then, gradually, he finds that his interest wanes, he becomes drowsy and distracted. Apathy and dissatisfied restlessness overcome him. His usual state of chronic boredom has returned. In time, the depression of boredom envelops him and he feels angry and dissatisfied with all of his world. He tries to pour his angry aggression into his work, and that is effective for a time, but finally he experiences the wish for another depreciated woman upon whom he can freely vent his wrath. And the cycle repeats.

For Donald, anger is not inextricably tied to sexuality, but aggressiveness is, as it must be for everyone. One must be clear about the distinction between anger and aggression. Angry behavior tends to be aggressive, but not all aggression is angry. Aggression refers to active assertion and, though it is sometimes prompted by anger, anger is not its necessary precondition. Sexual behavior always involves active assertion; loving another is always aggressive, but not angry.

Donald's internalized prohibition against assertive feelings associated with sexuality in the presence of a "good" woman resulted in the massive repression of those feelings in relation to his wife, contributing to his state of chronic boredom. The frustration of the blocked conscious experience and expression of those feelings created the pent-up rage that finally had to be vented upon some indifferent and depreciated woman. Once those angry and those self-assertive feelings were discharged, his chronic boredom was relieved for a time, but as his sexual tension built again, the cycle of boredom, depression, and anger would be repeated. It was not his wife's lack of sexual interest that created his boredom, although he attributed the blame to her. It was his own prohibition of active assertion of his sexual feelings toward her that created his boredom, and the frustration of that repression of feelings created the anger that came subsequently to be attached to those sexual feelings. Putting it another way, he did not hate women; he hated his own frustrating prohibition against active assertive sexual feelings, and this he mistakenly attributed to women.

A thorough examination of the intricacies of the emotional lives of the members of the C. family would entail an extensive treatise of its own, and that is not the present purpose. It is instead to portray through them the common theme of the search for feelings. Although they represent a range of ages, of character organization and temperament, of specific conventional psychopathology, the common theme of the search for feeling-fulness is present in all of them. Each attempts that quest in his own way. Susie tries mainly to substitute sensation for blocked feelings while Charlie prefers the Nietzschean pursuit of danger, evoking intensities of fear to break through his repressing barriers and satisfy his wish to feel intensely and, therefore, to feel alive. John ranges far and wide, seeking both sensation and feeling, seeking always to find something that will *feel* important to him. He calls his quest a search for himself, and in that he is quite correct, for he is trying always to get back in touch with his feeling self. Andrea pursues her own varied avenues, but mainly she attempts a return to the "joys of marital strife," neither to hurt nor to be hurt, but to be feelingfully involved with her husband once more in a way that had worked before. Donald seeks surcease from his boredom and depression in the company of depreciated "sexual technicians," not because they arouse his sexual desires, but because he can release his own inhibitions and consciously experience and express his already aroused but blocked feelings only in the specific circumstances of the presence of such women.

They are a busy lot, presenting a varied picture of restless striving activity not usually associated with states of boredom. There we expect to find apathy and inactivity, instead. The members of the C. family do experience longer or shorter periods of apathy and inactivity typically associated with boredom, but they have not given up the struggle, they have not slipped irretrievably into the specific apathetic depression so often caused by chronic boredom.

In the course of their development, each of them acquired an hypertrophied capacity to massively repress their feelings in the service of adaptation to external social demands. And each of them comes to an awareness at some point in his life that the price has been too great, that that route to social success has required an excessive sacrifice of personal experience and happiness. That awareness arises not in explicit form, but as a vague yet intense sense of something being wrong, of something missing. And then each, in his own way, seeks restitution, often blindly striving to recapture his lost capacity for feelingfulness.

That we have trouble in living with our feelings is a fact widely recognized and understood. It is far less recognized and very little understood that we have even greater trouble trying to live without them.

5

Transference: Defense Against Novelty

The desire to regulate our feeling-tension, to keep that tension within acceptable bounds, often leads us to use counterproductive measures against our feelings. Apparently, we are all close kin to the king who killed the messenger for although we cannot annihilate feelings in quite the same manner, we often attempt to approximate that act by avoiding our feelings in every way that we can. As previously described, we may avoid feelings by constricting life's experience to only those situations that would evoke little or no feeling. This avoidance leads to barren isolation or a life of dull routine. Repression, too, is a form of avoidance, the avoidance of conscious awareness of feelings that exist within us, which deprives us of the vital information feelings would bring.

Another form of avoidance that we use to defend ourselves is transference, a technique for avoiding the recognition of novelty in the external world, even when novelty is present, by creating the *illusion* of comfortable familiarity. The actual process of transference, simply described, is an unconscious distortion of perception in which a present object is misperceived as a significant object from the subject's past. A clear example of transference is to be found in a person who sees every authority figure as a reincarnation of his own cruel and autocratic father, or who sees in every woman he loves the repository of all his mother's charm, wit, beauty, and virtue.

My view of what brings this misperception about, the desire to avoid novelty, is a significant departure from traditional psychoanalytic thought.

THE MECHANISM OF TRANSFERENCE

Andrea C., at the outset of her treatment, saw me as a stranger, but also as a competent psychoanalyst who was able to be sympathetic, understanding, nonjudgmental and helpful. Some of that view was probably influenced by earlier positive experiences with others in helping professions but, by and large, I prefer to believe that she had a fairly accurate and objective perception of me. At any rate, it was fascinating to watch the multiple ways in which her perception of me changed from time to time during the course of her analysis, as it does with every patient undergoing this form of treatment. At one point she became angry with me and accused me of being moralistic and stuffy. She felt that I wanted all of her interest to be in me and that I would not allow her to have any interest in other men. What had happened to her earlier view of me as a nonjudgmental, sympathic, and understanding person?

The analyst must maintain a constant introspective vigil. Had I inadvertently allowed some of my own unconscious feelings to influence my attitude toward her? The analyst, too, is susceptible to transference distortion, albeit less susceptible than is the unanalyzed patient. Satisfied within myself that my attitude toward her had not changed, I was able to recognize that the way in which she now saw me coincided in remarkable ways with her earlier description of her father's attitudes toward her as a young teen-aged girl. At that time he had refused to let her date, go to mixed parties, wear lipstick, or dress attractively. He would not let her have any fun and she felt that he insisted that he was to be the only man in her life. It seemed that in my place she had constructed the image of her father of yore. And she tried to engage me in battle over these issues just as she had battled with her father many years ago. Those battles with her father were often tempestuous, reaching a crescendo of mutual rage and recrimination, followed by remorse and tearful reconciliation. Was this, perhaps, a basis for her attempts to relate to her husband through what she had termed "the joys of marital strife"?

This stormy episode in the analysis was resolved in timely fashion and Andrea thereby acquired some deeper knowledge and understanding of some of her characteristic behavior. But this experience did not, in itself, put an end to her tendency to periodically misperceive me. At times she attributed to me attitudes and behaviors that belonged more properly to her mother, and at other times intentions and feelings more correctly attributed to her younger sister. To misperceive me as father was one thing—at least age and gender were similar— but to see me as mother was stretching things further, and to see me as younger sister would be seen by most people to be almost bizarre. Yet, such events are common experience for the psychoanalyst who is able to read the historical message contained in these transference distortions.

The question confronting us is why such perceptual distortions occur. Why do reasonable people who possess the capacity for fairly accurate perception some of the time experience these episodes of extreme distortion?

When Freud recognized and named this phenomenon (1912), he realized its universality but he focused attention upon its particular effect as a resistance to the process of psychoanalysis. He pointed out that patients in analysis, following the basic rule of free association, would approach some nuclear conflict and fall silent, and that that silence was inevitably an attempt to avoid expression of some thought about the analyst that had arisen at that point. Such thoughts about the analyst were always to be understood as expressions of transference, peculiarly useful to the analyst capable of reading the message contained, for it revealed an unconscious memory in the patient of some aspect of his relationship to a significant person in his past.

Freud theorized that the purpose of transference was the unconscious reenactment of the past in an effort to avoid its conscious recollection. As I have said, my view differs, for I see the purpose of transference to be the avoidance of perceiving a novel present by calling up the old familiar images of the past. I maintain that most misperceptions, misunderstandings, preconceived notions, obsessive ideas and the like involve transference in an attempt to keep things familiar. This is an important point of difference, not only as it applies to the practical conduct of psychoanalysis, but also as it enlightens our broader understanding of man's fear of novelty.

Useful as transference is in the conduct of psychoanalysis, its disadvantage outside of that setting is immediately clear. Any distortion of perception poses a hazard, for we depend upon the accuracy of our perceptions to effectively cope with our world. Inaccurate perception may stem from other sources than transference. For example, impairment of the organs of perception may diminish visual and auditory acuity, but those impairments often may be corrected by glasses and hearing aids. No comparable mechanical devices are available to correct the distortions of transference.

Beyond these rather simple and direct examples of perceptual distortion the whole subject of the accuracy of perception of the external world is one filled with uncertainty. What do we mean by accurate perception and is such a thing even possible? The notion of distortion of perception clearly implies some standard of accuracy, yet we have moved far away from the naive idealism of Platonic times when it was thought that a fixed and certain reality existed out there and that it was objectively knowable by those of clear vision (perception). Philosophers like Locke and Descartes and Kant introduced and elaborated the notion of the limitations of man as the knower, and sought to find the answer to certain knowledge within the makeup of man himself. And in more recent times the linguists and the structuralists (Chomsky, Wittgenstein, et al.) have tied perception and knowledge of the real world to the development of language in man, attempting to demonstrate that man perceives what his language determines.

No doubt the philosophical discourse about reality and man's perception of it shall continue. As Platonic Idealism gave way to epistemology, hermeneutics, and the present trend of Deconstructionism, so we may surmise that other views of the matter will arise in their turn. Nor need we wait for some definitive resolution of the problem. Even accepting the limitations of man as perceiver and accepting that man may never be able to know the essential nature of reality, still he is able to perceive his world in a way that allows for adaptation. His knowledge of the nature of matter may be imperfect, but his perception is usually good enough to enable him to avoid colliding with walls. We are convinced that man need not perceive the essential nature of the universe in order to know that his wife is not his mother.

Were man's perceptual apparatus constructed along the lines of the electron microscope or machinery more sophisticated than we have yet conceived, he would perhaps come closer to perceiving his world in its essential form. But man must settle for his own construction, accepting the limits imposed upon his perception by that construction. The visual retina, for example, is limited in its response to specific wave lengths of electromagnetic energy, that segment of the spectrum which we call visible light. Nor is that retinal response to visible light transmitted directly to the mind as a visual image, ready-made. Instead, the activated retina sends neuronal impulses to the brain where those impulses are processed and an image is constructed. We are far from understanding the specific mechanisms by which the resulting image in the mind is constructed, but it is quite clear that the image constructed from a set visual stimulus may vary greatly among different viewers. The variety of responses to a stereotyped Rorschach ink blot stimulus is a simple example. And in that test the varied responses are used not to evaluate the registration of the light stimulus upon the retina, but primarily to evaluate the image construction subsequent to that registration. It is the process of construction of the image subsequent to retinal activation that is influenced by psychological factors in the individual, distorting the image that he constructs to greater or lesser degree. Whatever registers upon his perceptual apparatus may be perceived close to the registration or it may be distorted to accord with what he knows, what he anticipates, or what he wishes to be. For our purpose, accuracy of perception refers only to the closeness of the recognition to the registration, undistorted by anticipation or wish.

Even this sense of accuracy of perception may not be achievable in an absolute way, but within that context wide variations in degree of distortion between registration and recognition may occur. We may not be able to know the external world as that might appear to a truly objective knower, but whatever of the world registers upon our limited human apparatus, that we had better be able to recognize as clearly as we can.

Returning now to that form of perceptual distortion called transference, we understand that the problem lies not in the somatic apparatuses that register the sensations, but in some need of the subject to distort those registrations to conform with images from his past. Freud attempted to describe the dynamics of transference in terms of drives and their retained connection to images of those who provided gratification of the drives in the past (1912 p. 102). And this, in turn, he predicated upon a deeper principle that he proposed to call the repetition compulsion, a tendency in all things to return to an earlier state of being.

Freud advanced the speculative principle of the repetition compulsion in an effort to explain the apparent contradiction to his established belief in the dominance of the pleasure principle posed by transference. Under the sway of the pleasure principle man seeks pleasure and the avoidance of pain, but in the process of transference he often misperceives the present situation in terms of some painful experience from the past, and that seeming preference for pain required explanation. He proposed that the compulsion to repeat was actually an attempt to heal a past traumatic experience by gaining mastery of it in the repetition. And then he sought to ground this principle in his philosophical postulate of a fundamental death instinct, Thanatos, which existed along side and equal to the life instinct, Eros. Once more he established his dualism that determined the living of our lives: Eros, the life force that includes the pleasure principle, against Thanatos, the death instinct which leads us to our final goal of death and which includes the repetition compulsion. The concept of a death instinct has never gained wide acceptance, but the notion of a repetition compulsion remains deeply imbedded in psychoanalytic thought.

I see no reason to explain transference on the basis of some mysterious biologically grounded compulsion to repeat, for it can be explained at least equally well by the pleasure principle, for it simply involves a preference for a lesser pain than for an anticipated greater one. I do not believe that we are gripped by a fly-paper past, but that we do tend to run back to a familiar past when we are confronted by a novel and potentially uncomfortable or scary situation in the present. The mechanism is like that which operates in the young child spending his first night away from home, sleeping with his playmate who lives next door. He becomes frightened of the new surroundings, scared of the unfamiliarity of the situation, and must run back to his own house where everything is familiar and he feels secure. What is operative is not the grip of the past but the repulsion from the novel present. This explanation is not only more economical than Freud's but also leads to a much more promising approach to the correction of transference distortion.

When Andrea C. perceived me as a stand-in for her stuffy, possessive father, it was not because she was so fixated upon that image from the past that she could not perceive me clearly. After all, she was capable of a much clearer perception of me before and after that particular episode. It is rather the fact that she did see me as a real person toward whom she was beginning to have some very strong feelings that made her uncomfortable. I was still a relative stranger, someone she did not know very well. How would I react to her emerging strong feelings—what dangerous reactions might she anticipate from me? And how might she, herself, behave if these strong feelings did emerge into full conscious awareness? Would they move her to act in ways that would be shameful and humiliating or in some way dangerous to herself or to me? Fearful of the unknown consequences of her emerging feelings, she defensively and unconsciously constructed the image of her father in my place, thereby creating the illusion of comfortable familiarity. She knew her father very well. She had spent years growing up with him and, although she may not have been consciously aware of it, she knew his varied reactions in exquisite detail. She knew what was acceptable to him and what was not, what would please him and what would not. With her father in that room instead of me, she felt she knew precisely what feelings and behaviors she could permit herself.

In this way she resisted the temptation to allow her pressing feelings about me to emerge. That temptation was fostered by her accurate perception of my trustable neutrality. Trustable? That trust was still conditional. Experience had demonstrated that I remained quite neutral so far, but could she trust me to remain so under the pressure of her emerging strong feelings about me? She was not yet ready to take that risk and so, unconsciously, played it safe.

Within the context of the psychoanalytic process, this kind of perceptual distortion can be turned to advantage by the analyst who is keyed to the historical message it contains. But such is not the common mode of discourse between people, for they have an understandable expectation that the responses of others will accord, within limits, with who and what they are in the present. One can only imagine the myriad confusions that might attend an encounter between Bill and John when Bill misperceives John to be his father and

John misperceives Bill to be his younger brother. Then it would be as though a conversation were being carried on by four people, two of whom would be absent but represented in the unconscious minds of Bill and John, each unknown to the other. And yet, such confusing encounters are far from rare.

THE FEAR OF NOVELTY

What is so frightening about novelty, about the unanticipated and the unfamiliar that it leads to a defense in which the costly confusions of misperceptions are widely accepted by individuals for the sake of an illusion of familiarity? There is little difficulty in comprehending the fear of a novel situation that is life-threatening. The sophisticated urban dweller who suddenly finds himself alone in a tropical jungle, surrounded by predators, is ill-equipped to assure his very survival. And this fear for one's survival may be the root cause of the fear of novelty generally, but then it has extended far beyond the actual life-threatening situation, for the vastly preponderant fear of the novel involves far more mundane situations. Within the familiar contexts of our lives we tend often to have some fear of meeting new people, of encountering new situations, of seeing new things, and of learning new ways.

When called upon to cope with some new and unfamiliar situation the individual's task is twofold. He is called upon to perceive and assess the elements of that situation and to formulate an appropriate response. At the same time he must manage his own feelings that are evoked by the situation. These two tasks are usually lumped together as one, since they occur together and influence each other, but it will add clarity to our understanding to treat them as two quite separate tasks.

Perhaps this can best be illustrated by an old story. A foot traveler, lost in a blinding snow storm, finally stumbles by chance onto the edge of a small village where he is met by a number of local residents who take him into a home for food and warmth. Only then is he told that, coming from the direction that he did, he has just crossed several miles of thin ice covering the adjacent lake, and that he might have fallen through the icy crust and drowned at any step on the way. The traveler, hearing this, has a heart attack and dies, even though he is now on solid ground, warmed, and safe. What proved lethal in this instance was not the situation, but his feelings about the situation.

Considering a less threatening event, a teenager going to his first dance we see that the same conditions apply. He must engage an external task and an internal task simultaneously, and only by splitting it up in that way can we appreciate the balance of his effective function. His external task entails social affability with a young woman that he does not know very well, and he is supposed to dance with her with some degree of gracefulness. At the same time, he is probably experiencing many (internal) amorous and sexual feelings that are strong and unfamiliar. If he pays too much attention to where he is putting his feet while trying to dance gracefully, will he reveal his sexual feelings? Will he have an erection or accidentally touch her where he really wants to touch her? On the other hand, if he spends all of his attention on monitoring his feelings and his responses to them, then he probably will not be able to carry on much of a conversation with her, and may step all over her feet. As he is compelled to expend more effort on the internal task of monitoring his feelings, the less energy of attention will be available to him for the external task and, conversely, the more comfortable he is with his feelings, the less he will have to attend to them and the more he can attend to the external task.

Preponderantly, the fear of novelty reduces to the fear of one's own feelings. Although the fear is usually attributed to the novel external situation, what is operative is the fear of experiencing, and of having to handle, the impelling tension of unexpected and unfamiliar feelings evoked by that situation. And those feelings are feared because feelings impel us toward action, toward behavior that may be in some way dangerous or humiliating. Or if those feelings are contained, they may create degrees of tension that exceed our thresholds and cause unpleasure.

The Element of Surprise

Freud considered surprise to be the condition that distinguished fright from fear (1920), and it played an important role in his concept of trauma, a condition in which the nervous system becomes overwhelmed by an influx of stimulation greater than its ability to manage. He theorized that where a perceptual system was charged with a certain energy, it had a greater capacity to "bind" inflowing excitation and thereby could protect the nervous system from being overwhelmed. Many present-day critics reject this notion as an example of "neurologizing psychology," as being too physicalist and simplistic. Even so, modern neurophysiology is discovering interesting things about the chemistry of neuronal synaptic transmission that may well lead to the discovery of neurological processes that correlate with Freud's psychological thesis.

Leaving the uncertain theoretical discussion of specific physiological mechanisms aside, some things are quite apparent at a purely phenomenological level. An intense, sudden, and unexpected stimulus will evoke a startle reaction while that same stimulus when anticipated will not do so. There is something about the state of readiness, of preparedness, that helps to diminish the impact of a stimulus. On the other hand, a state of high feeling-tension can intensify the impact of a lesser stimulus, one that would not cause a startle reaction in that individual in a lower tension state.

Novelty, by its very nature, promises surprise. Newness precludes anticipation; one lacks guidelines from experience by which to prepare one's self. One cannot know precisely what stimuli will occur nor what feelings may be evoked. Not only is there a lack of preparation, but the apprehension of facing novelty creates a heightened tension state so that even lesser stimuli and less-intense evoked feelings tend to have a greater impact than in lesser tension states. And so we seek to avoid novelty and surprise, even at the cost of misperceiving present reality.

What remains troublesome is the notion of accuracy of perception. One could quite correctly argue that any person with truly accurate perception would encounter nothing but novelty, for no encountered event is precisely a repetition of any prior event; there is always something new. Such a person would live in a constant state of surprise, always assessing her novel conditions, formulating her responses and, at the same time, handling her own evoked feelings. Some would describe her, then, as heading inevitably toward madness, while others would describe her as a truly creative being. The vast majority of us face life with something less than this ultimate accuracy, however, imposing an order, a regularity, upon the events of our lives by glossing over differences and stressing sim-ilarities. There is economic saving in that approach, for then we need not reconstruct our world every time we encounter some small novelty. But significant novelty, novelty that makes a difference, does matter, and we court disaster when our need to keep our world constant leads us to misperceive it.

The need to keep the world constant acts as a deterrent to change and accounts for the high degree of inertia encoun-tered in the course of human events. Those who refuse to tolerate the surprise of unanticipated feelings cling stubbornly to established ways and tenaciously resist all new ideas—their own as well as those of others. Not only is their own creativ-ity severely curtailed but they reject the valuable creative contributions of others out of hand. People of differing cultures encounter each other with suspicion and discomfort, and provincialism is perpetuated. Resistance to novelty will even make it difficult for many to entertain the notion that human beings can be viewed in a better light and that they are capable of being better than they believe themselves to be.

The encounter with novelty promises, or threatens, surprise from two sides: the unknown and unanticipated circumstances of the external reality and the unpredictable evoked feelings within. He who is most familiar with the whole range of feelings, in terms of both variety and intensity, is least likely to be surprised by the evocation of those feelings. One cannot be familiar with the external novelty, by definition, but one can be quite familiar with one's self. He who achieves a high level of self-familiarity approaches external novelty with little trepidation. He is self-confident. For him it is only the external situation that carries potential surprise, and then it often becomes the kind of surprise that delights.

6

The Centrality of Love

Love has a central significance for man. It has been a primary preoccupation of philosophers, poets, theologians, writers, and psychologists throughout history. However, although we intuitively understand love's importance at a deep level, we do not trust it. What is there about love that renders us so vulnerable, that makes us so guarded about its experience and expression? We seem to be loving creatures who have learned to be afraid to love.

The central position that love holds requires that we shift the focus of this discussion. The preceding chapters have attempted to examine and understand the ways and means by which we seek to avoid or to minimize the tension of our feelings in general, and the price we pay for those efforts. Now we must focus upon this specific feeling of love to try to understand not only what it is and why it is so important in human life, but why we often employ any and all of those means to resist a feeling that we so value and desire.

While the nature of love has been explored by man through the ages, we have yet to understand the phenomenon. Some things about love are pretty much agreed upon: it is a feeling, it is impelling, and it appears in man quite universally. It is generally valued, both experientially and morally. And it is "blind". But what more can we say about love with any degree of conviction? What more do we know about its origin, its operation, its significance?

To undertake yet another exploration of the nature of love

is a venture that inspires a certain feeling of dread. Can it prove to be anything but futile? Can it be done without falling into all of the old cliches and sentimental generalizations? On the other hand, can one justify avoiding the effort? It would be especially difficult for me to duck the issue because my work has shown me that most of man's psychological ills are clustered around his fear of loving, and I place even greater importance on love than do many.

Much of what I have to say on the subject of love is speculative; an attempt to construct a feasible hypothesis. And my justification for such speculation is simply the absence of a working hypothesis to explain this feeling that is of such central importance to any thorough understanding of man.

THE DYNAMICS OF LOVE

I suggest that love is interest; an intense expression of interest, to be sure, but interest all the same. To love is to be intensely interested in; not interested about, not interested for, but interested *in*. By that I mean that interest is given. It is not contingent upon repayment or return. In that sense, love is generous, and it is universally human; a trait of all people everywhere. This does not mean that people are universally loving and generous, that everyone loves everyone and everything. Experience quickly dispels the idealized image of a world filled with people intensely and generously interested in all. That loving is a universal trait means, at best, that everyone has a tendency to love someone or some thing even though toward the rest of the world one may be quite indifferent, even hostile or greedy. Further, if some people appear to love only themselves, that emotion is still love and must be included in our description.

However, the assertion of a conclusion, that love is interest, is hardly sufficient. We must start at the beginning; love is a feeling. Since I have taken the position that feelings are always a reflection of some disequilibrium in man's interacting systems, we must first attempt to link the feeling of love, or interest, to some particular disequilibrium. One particular aspect of love, its tendency to be constant, suggests that we are searching for a form of disequilibrium that also tends to be equally constant. In that way it seems to be different from other feelings that derive from physiological disequilibrium. Hunger and sexual desire, as examples, are feelings that derive from specific physiological disequilibriums, feelings that impel toward action directed to the restoration of equilibrium; one eats and hunger is dissipated, one has sexual intercourse and sexual desire is dissipated, at least for a period of time. Certainly those disequilibriums will recur and their reflective feelings will return. But such periodicity is not typical of the feeling of love. One does not find that the feeling of love is even temporarily dissipated once it is expressed in action (i.e. intense interest in the love object). Instead, there seems to be a continuous source for the feeling.

In searching for a continuous disequilibrium that might be the source of love I shall turn to Freud's explanation of the source of instincts in the somatic processes of the body (1915 c.) The one somatic process that is relatively constant and continuous is our general metabolism, a necessary corollary of existence. I propose that this is the source of the feeling of interest, the most intense form of which is love.

What is so far lacking in this attempt at explanation is anything that suggests the disequilibrium that we require as a source of a feeling. However, when we turn to Franz Alexander's concept of surplus energy (1948), the matter takes on a different coloration. His is a concept that has never been fully integrated into psychoanalytic theory, yet it has never quite gone away, either. He states,

"From the point of view of energy, life can be viewed as a relationship between three vectors: the intake of energy in the nutritive substances and oxygen; their partial retention for use in growth; and the expenditure of energy to maintain existence, its loss in waste, in heat, and in erotic playful activities. . . . Energy which is not needed to maintain life in equilibrium is called here surplus energy. This is the source of all sexual activity."

Freud employed the term, libido, to refer to a fundamental instinct that was the basis of love and of sexuality, and which derived from somatic processes. It is, of course, closely related to Alexander's concept of surplus energy as the source of sexual activity, but Alexander's way of stating it allows us to recognize that there is a disequilibrium involved; a *surplus* of energy arising from our general metabolic function. It is a disequilibrium that, under ordinary circumstances, would tend to be relatively constant and continuous, satisfying our particular requirements. Freud pointed out that when there is physical illness, for example, there is a corresponding diminution of libido, and that fits with Alexander's concept for if all of one's energy is being used for the maintenance of life in equilibrium, there would be no surplus energy, no source for sexual activity. In the terms of the thesis that I am suggesting there would be a corresponding diminution of interest and love.

If there is such a nice correlation between Freud's concept of libido, Alexander's concept of surplus energy and sexuality, and my proposed concept of interest and love, why then was there any need for me to undertake my exploration in the first place? Why was it not sufficient for me to subsume the feelings of interest and love, as Freud and Alexander do, under Freud's concept of libido and Alexander's elaboration of libido in his concept of surplus energy? The reason lies in the close connection made by both Freud and Alexander between love and sexuality, a connection that has been assumed to be fixed and established but which I see to have little basis. It is that firm connection between love and sexuality that has been a fundamental source of error and confusion in psychoanalytic thought, leading to the need to explain friendship, for example, as the expression of a desexualized or neutralized libido. Interest, too, must then be explained away as an expression of libido that has been changed in some way, and love of one's parents or children or friends is assumed to carry with it some sexuality, at least in hidden form. Sublimation, neutralization, desexualization of libido all come to look like epicycles on a pre-Copernican map of the solar system, ad hoc theories attempting to correct for discrepancies in the basic theory.

Love and Sex

The idea of separating love and sex is not new. C. G. Jung (1916) took exception to Freud's concept of the sexual basis of libido, proposing that sexuality was only one of its expressions. Jung saw libido to be a "general interest" and related it to Schopenhauer's Will and Bergson's "elan vital." It was Jung's disagreement with Freud that led to the historical split between the two men. Some years later, Jung (1936) wrote,

> "I do not mean to deny the importance of sexuality in psychic life, though Freud stubbornly maintains that I do deny it. What I seek is to set bounds to the rampant terminology of sex which threatens to vitiate all discussion of the human psyche; I wish to put sexuality itself in its proper place. Common-sense will always return to the fact that sexuality is only one of the life instincts; only one of the psycho-physiological functions; though one that is without doubt very far-reaching and important."

There is a strong link between love and sex in conventional thought, but we must be careful to separate those feelings that have an intrinsic connection from those feelings that become connected by the imposition of man's moral values. The connection between love and sex, like that between marriage and sex, is a connection imposed by man, expressing one view of how to best maintain social order. Some argue that sex and love must be connected because sex is so much better with someone you love, but that argument is not very convincing. Many things are much better when done with someone you love. Having dinner or taking a walk in the woods is better when you're with someone you love, but that doesn't cement the activities of dining or walking in the woods to love in the same way that convention attempts to bind sex to love.

On the other hand, there are plenty of arguments in favor of the separation of sex and love. The venerable history of prostitution, the prevalence of promiscuous, recreational sex, and indeed, the prevalence of rape and other forms of sexual expression that have a clear connection with hostility, not with love, all are strong arguments against any intrinsic connection between sex and love.

In the Introduction, I have expressed my dissatisfaction with the limitations imposed upon us by Freud's drive theory. The reduction of man's motivation to two fundamental and opposing forces, libido and aggression, may have satisfied Freud's wish to establish a simple basis for explaining the prevalence of conflict in mental life, but I believe it is unnecessary and confusing. Conflict may arise from any number of opposing forces, not just two, and when one arbitrarily compresses all of those opposing forces into two main camps one inevitably creates many strange bedfellows. Love is *forced* to become allied with sex, just as anger and destructiveness are forced into alliance with aggressiveness and assertiveness. Assertiveness may be angry, but it need not be, and sex may be loving, but it is not always so. Freud's reductionism forced artificial amalgams of unrelated feelings that created more confusion than clarity, for then additional theories had to be invented to explain the existence of many of those feelings when they appeared totally divorced from their supposed roots.

Much greater explanatory clarity can be achieved by accepting the complexity of man's motivational mechanism; that is, by accepting the variety of his feelings, each reflecting some disequilibrium in one of his interacting systems, and each impelling him to act to restore equilibrium. This provides us with a theory of motivation while leaving us free to examine the full range of man's complexity.

To restate my proposition, then, I suggest that interest and its most intense form of expression, love, is the feeling that reflects a disequilibrium in terms of a surplus of energy deriving from our general metabolic function. In rather unromantic terms, it is a psychological byproduct of our metabolism, comparable to the production of heat in an ongoing exothermic chemical reaction. Pursuing that analogy, as long as the chemical reaction goes on, heat is being produced, and something must be done with that heat; it must be expended. So, too, interest is constantly being generated within us and it, too, must be expended, which accounts for the universal search of man for someone or something to be interested in; to love.

I have suggested that love and interest are the central and most pervasive of all of man's feelings, and we see in the above explanation some theoretical substantiation of that view. While feelings like hunger and sexual desire reflect episodic disequilibriums in particular and discrete physiological systems, love is a feeling that reflects a continuous process that involves our total physiological organization. But for many of us theory is not enough; we require more direct evidence to be convinced. Then let us turn to experience and question what is life like without interest, without love. Life then becomes mere existence, dull and tedious, devoid of color. We are reminded of the plight of the chronically bored who, cut off from their feelings, seek desperately for intensity so that life might become interesting once more.

Man, then, is an interested and loving creature, a creature that generates an unending supply of interest, love, that he is impelled to expend, that he wishes to give generously. What stops him so often from doing so, then? The broad answer is fear of unpleasureable consequences.

The Centrality of Love

Love and Interest

Before pursuing that complicated subject, however, it remains to elaborate the connection of interest to love. If it could be proven that love is an intense form of interest, have we gained anything thereby? If love is interest, then what is interest? It is all well and good to say that interest is simply what Freud meant by libido but without the sexual basis he attributed to that concept, or that it is a cathexis, a charge of energy that we attach to things, again as Freud described it, but those explanations remain abstractions, distant from our experience.

We are stuck with language that seems to demand that concepts be defined or described in terms of other concepts that are often equally elusive. But perhaps there is one experiential phenomenon that we can connect to the concept of interest and that is attention, by which we mean a focused awareness. It is a universal experience that it takes a lot of effort to pay attention to anything that does not hold your interest while it is quite effortless to attend to something that you are interested in. Indeed, it requires much effort to not attend to that which is interesting. Then it is clear that interest and attention, while not at all synonymous, are tightly connected. It is interest that directs our attention, our focused conscious *and unconscious* awareness (viz., the sleeping mother of a newborn infant sleeps through the raucous traffic noise outside her window but quickly awakens at her infant's first whimper).

The connection of interest to attention poses a dilemma, however. Consider the hiker in the woods who encounters a rattlesnake a short distance away. His attention will certainly be drawn to it and, I daresay, it would require a good deal of effort of him to not pay attention to it. Are we to infer, then, that the hiker loves this venomous creature? It is most unlikely. If we compare the hiker's interest in the snake to that of a herpetologist in a similar creature, we immediately recognize a difference. The herpetologist is truly interested in the snake itself, while the hiker's interest is in himself, in his own safety, and his apparent interest in the snake is merely an extension of his interest in his own integrity. The hiker would be most pleased to have missed this encounter entirely while the herpetologist might quite reasonably be expected to be out searching for the creature. What determines the difference is the attitude of generosity. The herpetologist is interested in the snake itself, while the hiker's interest is contingent—i.e., he would have little or no interest in the snake if his own safety were not threatened by it.

In summary, then, the working hypothesis that I sought to develop earlier in this chapter is that love is intense interest generously given, accompanied by effortless attention to the love object. Each person is a constant generator of feelings of interest and love reflecting a surplus energy created by his metabolic activity which must be expended to maintain equilibrium. From this we should expect that loving would be an easy thing to do, we should expect to see love spontaneously manifested all around us, but experience does not generally accord with those expectations. Although we occasionally encounter individuals who appear to be intensely interested in things and who are spontaneously loving, the far larger numbers of people we see have a great deal of difficulty in loving. They tend to be very cautious about it—even stingy with it— and we wonder why they are so conservative with feelings that have such a continuous source.

Fear of Rejection

The major stumbling block to loving is the fear of rejection, but we must try to understand why rejection of one's love is felt to be so painful. The conventional view holds that rejection means a failure to win the desired love of the other and that it is this failure of the wish to be loved in return that is so painful. That view places primary emphasis on the wish to be loved and relegates the desire to love to a secondary,

The Centrality of Love

instrumental role—the means for achieving love from others. But the view here presented is that the wish to love is primary and that, while being loved is pleasurable, loving is also pleasurable in and of itself, and can be treated independently of any wish to be loved in return.

Then to understand the pain of the rejection of one's love we must examine what goes on in the person who is loving. To say that one loves another is to say that he is intensely interested in that person and, as he is interested in that person, so his attention is automatically and effortlessly given to that person. The loved one becomes a focus of his attention, just as his self has been a focus of his attention. This does not require a diminution of his interest in or attention to himself but involves an expansion of his interest and attention to two centers of his being. Now he is concerned with his loved one's wishes and feelings as he is concerned with his own. It is this generosity that is often viewed as self-sacrifice and in extreme situations may even eventuate in the forfeiture of his own existence in favor of the loved one's. And it is this generosity that is experienced as "giving one's self to another."

The rejection of one's love is experienced, then, as the rejection of one's self. Were it only feelings of love rejected, that would be of lesser consequence, but because of the equation of one's love with one's self, it is one's self that is deemed to be unworthy of acceptance. In the light of the earlier discussion of self-esteem, it becomes clear that those with low self-esteem will experience loving as a risky undertaking. They approach loving with trepidation for they start with the conviction that the self they have to offer is not worth very much, and rejection becomes a confirmation of their low self-valuation. Those with high self-esteem can love more freely for, although rejection of their love is painful, too, it is less so for their self-esteem does not depend upon the acceptance of others.

The failure of the wish to be loved in return is not the basis of the pain of rejection. One may love many things without any expectation of being loved in return. You may love your work, or nature, or a musical composition—inanimate things that are incapable of returning love. There may be rewards involved, but often the love of those things is reward enough. The wish to be loved may appear to be more prevalent than the wish to love, but that is illusory. When one recognizes the relationship of love and interest, then it becomes clear that the wish to be interested in people and things, to find something that is "meaningful," to feel intensely committed to something, are all expressions of the far more prevalent desire to love. Beyond that, there is the common confusion of love and esteem, previously described, that leads many to express a wish to be loved when they really mean that they want to be esteemed, and this in the hope of compensating for their own low self-esteem. But perhaps the most significant reason for the apparent prevalence of the expressed wish to be loved is the fear of loving. Here the wish to be loved is the wish for a guarantee in advance that one's own love will be accepted.

The pain of rejected love lies not in the failure to be loved in return but in the failure to be esteemed by the one you love. By loving that person you have elevated the importance of his feelings, wishes, and *judgments* to a level equal to your own. Therein lies the vulnerability of the lover who, by his gift of love, empowers another to judge the lover's worth and gives it equal weight with his own self-evaluation. That is the power that the lover gives to his loved one. People tend to be very cautious about giving that kind of power to anyone, and that in large measure explains why the fear of loving is so widespread.

The wish to be valued by a loved person is but an extension of the desire for self-approval that is strong in everyone. The acceptance of your love is a statement of its value to the person you love and, since one's love is equated with one's self, it is a statement that *you* are valued by your loved one. This reinforcement of one's self-esteem is a large part of the reason that the accepted lover feels so good. But as one's love is rejected, so one's self-esteem falls. Those with high self-esteem are more willing to take the risk of loving even though

The Centrality of Love

the rejection of their love will be hurtful. For them, at least, it is a split vote: one nay and one yea, so to speak. Those with low self-esteem have nothing to fall back upon. Rejection of their love constitutes a unanimous decision that they have little or no value.

Love and Intimacy

More significant than any connection between love and sexuality is the strong connection between love and the desire for intimacy, which also relates to the wish to be esteemed by one you love. Sexuality is only one possible form of intimacy between people, but loving carries with it a desire for openness and sharing in all realms of experience. The wish to be open and unguarded seems strange for we are far more often inclined to be secretive about our inner thoughts and feelings. But perhaps that in itself is the impetus toward intimacy. In the rest of life we expend a good deal of effort to present to the world an external appearance that is largely defined by convention, and to hide from general view all those things that conventional experience teaches us to keep secret. A loving relationship is like a sanctuary then, a place where you can relax your guard and seek to be esteemed for who and what you really are.

There is little value in being esteemed for who and what you *pretend* to be. That creates only the conviction that you have fooled another one. That may be alright for the rest of the world, for their opinions don't carry that much weight. But the judgments of those you love do matter, and to gain their esteem by guile avails nothing.

High self-esteem is important, then, not only in allowing one to love, but also in enabling one to maintain and deepen loving relationships. Many such relationships founder on this issue, for those who do not think well of themselves will tend to be guarded and secretive even with a loved one, hoping thereby to preserve the relationship. The resulting failure of intimacy, however, creates a void that is often not recognized for what it is, while causing deep discontent.

The importance of the feeling of love cannot be over-emphasized, for much of our discontent relates directly to our difficulty in loving well. What we see on the surface is the stinginess and greed of people who seem to want everything for themselves, and we too often fail to recognize that surface picture as a distortion, a result of inhibited and frustrated generosity and love. That picture leads us to treat love with a certain cynicism, a disbelief in its validity, and to take the "practical" view that man is by nature hostile and greedy. There seems an abundance of evidence in favor of that view: wars, crime, other forms of man's inhumanity to man. And those who believe in man's loving nature are thought to be only cockeyed optimists. But deep within each of us, no matter how secretly, each knows how he longs to love some-one, something, and how life takes on a brighter hue as he succeeds in doing so. We guard against the vulnerability of loving, but the impetus to love is very strong and often overcomes the resistance, at least partially. And so most end up loving, but not well, confounded by their efforts to protect themselves.

Fear of Loving

We are afraid to trust our loving feelings for they render us so vulnerable to rejection and to the loss of self-esteem that entails. Those who try to protect themselves from such loss by repression of their loving feelings lose touch with their feelings of interest, as well, for there is no clear boundary between interest and love. Then they are left with lives that lack interest and they feel empty and bored. Life, for them, holds little meaning (significance), and they desperately seek to regain contact with life's intensity, pursuing sensations to replace lost feelings or exposing themselves to potential disas-ter in an effort to break through their self imposed internal barriers against the experience of feelings. As previously described, this state of chronic boredom sets the stage for the development of the specific depression of chronic boredom or for the hysterical and obsessive-compulsive neuroses that have become more commonly recognized.

No wonder, then, that I hold that most of man's psychological ills cluster around his fear of loving. It is not that man fears *only* his feelings of love and interest; he fears the intensity of other feelings, as well. Sometimes he is afraid of his anger, his exhibitionism, his curiosity, his humiliation; the list can go on and on. But when he loses touch with his interest, his love, then he has lost touch with the most constant and pervasive of all of his feelings, and that is the most grievous loss of all.

The resistance against loving is often only partially successful, and then these people usually end up loving, but they encounter all of the difficulties in loving that spring from their excessive need to protect themselves. It is a practical impossibility to describe and explain every form of love gone awry. Perhaps each person has his own unique tale to tell, but at least certain broad outlines can be drawn.

First comes the demand for a guarantee of acceptance in advance, usually taking the form of an insistence upon being loved before venturing to love in return. And the more cautious the lover, the more insistent will he be on constant reassurance that he is loved more than he will allow himself to love. He convinces himself, thereby, that he holds the upper hand, that he will not be rejected. But such love becomes demanding, not generous, and this grudging withholding seriously interferes with the intimacy that love itself requires.

Some prefer to love things rather than people, and the reason for that is clear. Things cannot form judgments, and things can be possessed. One feels secure, in control, of a loved thing that is possessed. And so we find the common association of possessiveness with love for people as well. It is not that possessiveness is part of loving nor is it necessarily associated with it, but it is, again, a defensive operation in the insecure. This insecurity and resultant possessiveness gives rise to the notion, in romanticized form, that two people in love must be as one. That is but a thinly disguised expression of the wish to possess another person to assure constancy of acceptance. Such "loving" is not generous but is always contingent upon compliance.

It is one matter to possess things, but an entirely different matter to possess another person. Possession of another person is, in brief, a matter of slavery, and few possessive lovers would be willing to admit that the imposition of slavery is their intent. Instead, they often seek out very dependent people to love, people whose extreme dependency forces slavishness upon them. Then the possessive lover feels secure in his control while he believes himself to be exonerated from any accusation of imposing that control upon the other. But the dependent loved one will resent that control and resentment, even hatred, becomes an adulterant to love.

Another expression of possessive love may be seen in those who are quite able to love their very young children but who are incapable of loving a peer, or even their own children when they have grown older and less dependent. This love of very dependent people is the expression of the common wish to be needed, presumably based upon the premise that if one is sufficiently needed by another one is pretty well guaranteed acceptance.

The lover who is himself very dependent has often confused dependency with love. Because he feels that he *needs* the other person, he convinces himself that he loves that person. Then he acts loving to secure his dependent need, but that is only an act, not a true expression of loving feelings. It is often simply the price paid for the return of things needed.

There is in this no effort to deny the interdependency of people, no matter how mature they may be. But there is a great difference between the mature person who depends upon others for the satisfaction of his wants and those less mature who mistake wants for needs. The source of this confusion of love and dependency lies mainly in the early period of human development when the young child is simultaneously loving and dependent. How the vicissitudes of development may promote this confusion will be further elaborated in Chapter 8.

We are far from the limits of man's ingenuity in protecting himself from the vulnerability of loving. Another common device is transference distortion, which enables the lover to perceive—to misperceive—his loved one as being just like someone from the lover's past.

It is relevant to note at this point that Freud described only two types of object choice in loving—the anaclitic (leaning on) and the narcissistic (1914, pp. 187–88). In the first, one loves a person reminiscent of those upon whom one was once dependent (parent); in the second, one loves a person who is like one's self. The article in which this is described strongly suggests that these are the only choices, but whether or not that was Freud's intent, that is the impression that has influenced conventional psychoanalytic thought. And that is an impoverished view of man's capacity for love, leaving no room for understanding more mature and generous expressions of love that are at least occasionally encountered. The anaclitic and narcissistic choices are certainly frequent, but they are not inevitable. Instead, they are to be understood as protective operations of those who seek to defend themselves against the novelty and uniqueness of those they love.

He who is afraid to love, afraid to empower another to judge him as he judges himself, tries to play it safe by loving someone who is like someone else who has already demonstrated some degree of acceptance for him. And that is usually a parent or himself. Of course it is quite impossible to find someone who fits the image exactly, so one settles for suggestive similarities and then uses those as a basis for creating an unconscious distorted image that does fit the past image more precisely. Trouble then arises whenever the reality of the loved person does not fit with the lover's defensively distorted image of him. Then the lover feels hurt, disappointed, betrayed.

Some others are afraid to go even that far, afraid to trust

even those similarities that they, themselves, have created and so they love only themselves. These are the truly narcissistic characters who, because of their distrust, will invest in no one outside of themselves.

And still others will not love at all. These are the chronically bored that I have previously described. It is my impression that they have made their unconscious choice at a very young age; not so young that they have never experienced love and interest for, then, how could they miss it so?; but at a time when they were young enough to not know the full consequences of their decision. Then they spend the rest of their lives attempting to rediscover life, not ever clearly comprehending what is missing.

Love and Self-Esteem

To love, to be intensely interested in people and things, is not just a moral prescription nor a cultural view of how people should behave because that's a good way to be. It is a pervasive *feeling* that is integral to the human organism; man *must* love because loving is a central function of his being. Self-esteem, one's judgement of one's self, is a measure of how well one exercises all of one's inherent functions.

Failure to love, and to love well, lowers self-esteem; at the same time, low self-esteem seriously lowers one's capacity to love well, creating fear of venturing love and constricting the capacity for intimacy. The situation seems to present a circularity to which only freedom from fear of one's feelings can provide an answer.

Our quest for happiness must begin within ourselves. That goal requires, first, that one feel good about one's self, and that can only happen when each person is able and willing to accept his own feelings, and is confident of his ability to behave well (in accord with his judgement and his cultural values) in response to his feelings. Then that person has achieved autonomy.

7

Autonomy: Man's Best Hope for Happiness

Individual development is a story of the struggle for self-mastery. Every person starts life as a helpless and totally dependent being and continues in a state of relative helplessness throughout infancy and childhood. It is as though, having suffered the insult of helplessness, he then spends the rest of his life trying to achieve autonomy. Total success in that effort is an ideal rarely—perhaps never—achieved, yet we each approach that goal to some greater or lesser degree. The conscious recognition that that is our goal and a clear view of what that goal looks like should facilitate our efforts to approach it ourselves and—through our adoption of reasonable child care practices (suggested in Chapter 8)—enhance our children's efforts as well.

CHOICE AND DETERMINISM

It is difficult to reconcile the notion of autonomy with the explicitly deterministic view inherent in psychoanalytic theory. The view that all psychic events are determined (albeit,

Autonomy: Man's Best Hope for Happiness

with all the complexity of multiple determinants) seems incompatible with the idea that one has freedom of choice, that one is capable of volition, that one is, indeed, master of one's self. Those who hew strictly to the determinism line claim that free will is an illusion, that we only think we are making choices while in actuality heredity and experience set our choices for us inflexibly. We cannot dismiss the evidence in favor of determinism—the human mind conceives the world in terms of cause and effect. We strive always to understand cause–effect relationships and that effort has rewarded us with a great deal of scientific and technologic progress. When events occur without apparent cause–effect explanations, we feel helpless and afraid and we will even resort to mythologic and superstitious explanations to restore some sense of comfort. For example, saying "Such is God's will. . . ." or calling the event an "act of fate." What is most interesting is that the lack of such explanation evokes helplessness and fear, while the conviction of understanding cause and effect creates a feeling of mastery. The understanding need not be accurate to create the feeling of mastery; it requires only a sense of personal conviction.

It is strange that this conviction of understanding creates a sense of mastery, even when that understanding is more rather than less accurate. For example, it comforts us to know that objects fall to earth because of the existence of a force that we call gravity, yet knowing it does not exert any influence at all upon that force of gravity. We do not become masters of gravity by knowing its effect upon objects. But that is not the point. Knowing about gravity does not make us masters of gravity, but it does make us more masters of ourselves in relation to gravity. It helps to create for us an ordered universe in which we can anticipate related events and so accommodate our own behavior instead of being constantly surprised and bewildered by the unexpected.

This distinction between the wish to be masters of ourselves and the wish to be masters of the external world, of things and of others, is in some ways a subtle one that often gets lost—as it did in Adlerian psychology. There the will to mastery ambiguously embraced both, and when that happens the more central and significant wish to be master of one's self becomes submerged or sidetracked in the frenetic bustle to secure one's position in relation to the external world.

Understanding causes does not make us master of those causal forces, but it does enhance our mastery of ourselves in relation to those forces. Not only is this true in relation to gravity, lightning, and flood, but it applies equally to knowing and understanding those motivating forces within us, our feelings. The more we know our feelings directly and consciously, the greater is our conviction that we are the active agents of our choices.

One man, having completed a messy task, washes his hands. He does so for reasons of aesthetics and sanitation, and he thinks that this is a volitional act born of his own choice. But since all psychic events are determined, can this act be a free choice? Had he been born to another culture with different aesthetic values and no knowledge of sanitation, his choice would have been differently determined. Perhaps, then, his conviction of volition and choice is illusory. Compare him, however, with another man, a compulsive hand-washer. He, too, washes his hands, but he washes his hands every fifteen or twenty minutes, whether they are messy or not. His act is determined, as well, but he does not know why he does it, he knows only that he is compelled to do it. Is there truly no difference in volition and choice in these two examples? The first knows his feelings and his reasons and has employed his judgment, and although his judgment was totally determined by his heredity, history, and the present situation, still it was *his* judgment, his own *unique* judgment.

The second man did not act upon his judgment—indeed, his judgment might have been quite contrary, seeing this hand-washing to be absurd and intrusive. Yet he was compelled to proceed with the action. He does not feel that he is the active agent of his action, but instead, as George Groddek (1923) put it, experiences it as being lived by unknown forces.

Autonomy: Man's Best Hope for Happiness

There is a difference between the two cited instances, a difference, at least in degree, of conscious awareness of causes or reasons and the use of judgment. He who is consciously aware of motives and acts in accordance with his judgement (no matter that that judgment is determined) experiences himself as autonomous, while he who lacks consciousness of motives and is compelled to act without, or despite, his judgment, sees himself as helplessly driven. It is the conscious awareness of motivating feelings and the conscious use of rational judgment (trial action based upon knowledge and experience) that determines the experience of autonomy.

This emphasis on the consciousness of the experience appears to be at odds with conventional wisdom, which often recommends that a person dealing with a difficult choice had best "sleep on it," thereby affirming the proposition that unconscious and preconscious processes play a most significant role in decision making. Freud observed long ago that only the most superficial and trivial decisions were reached by logic and intellect alone. That is not the point, however. I do not claim at this point that he who is conscious of his motivations and consciously uses his judgment necessarily makes better or more accurate decisions, but only that he experiences the decision reached as being his own rather than a mysterious product of inspiration, luck (good or bad), or even of divine intervention.

Most creative people are notably poor at explaining the processes by which they have arrived at their successful endeavors, processes that are largely unconscious and preconscious, and they are the most prone to attribute their success to the muse, feeling themselves to be only a vehicle through which some mysterious force finds expression. We value their productions no less for that, but they do not see themselves as the autonomous creators of their work, and their next undertaking will tend to be filled with the same uncertain turmoil as was their last.

If conscious awareness of motivations and conscious use of judgment do not make for better choices, better decisions, then what is the use of it? First of all, it does create a sense of autonomy, which is worthwhile in and of itself. But beyond that I would argue that consciousness does make for better choices. A problem arises when one pits conscious knowledge and judgment against preconscious and unconscious mental processes—when one determines to "go with the facts and not with the feelings" (as though one's feelings were not facts pertinent to the situation!), or, conversely, to go with the feelings, ignoring the facts of the situation. To be conscious of motivation is to be conscious of one's feelings, to give them credence, to understand that they constitute data on a par with all the other "factual" data to be considered. It is not an "either-or" proposition but a realization that the broadest consideration of all the data available will probably lead to the most felicitous choice, and "all of the data available" includes the clearest possible perception of the facts of the present situation (with the least transference distortion), the most immediate awareness of one's feelings (minimal blocking of affect), and a clear knowledge of one's personal history that contributes to those present feelings (minimal repression of memory).

This is the goal toward which psychoanalysis as a therapy directs itself. There is, however, one other relevant issue that requires elucidation. Cast in classical psychoanalytic language, the problem of choice is usually posed in terms of conflict between impulse and reality, between "pleasure principle" and "reality principle," between the id (repository of the drives) and the ego (which perceives reality). This is too narrow a focus, for the superego, whose conscious manifestation is conscience, is usually left out of the discussion, probably because the conscience is overvalued as a keeper of peace and order. What would this world be like if people didn't have their consciences to keep them in line!

Well, it is not a matter of doing away with superego, with conscience, for that is probably an impossible feat. Everyone growing up in a culture inevitably absorbs the values and attitudes inherent in that culture and that is not, in itself, a bad thing. But in large measure the superego operates unconsciously, and to be driven by one's unconscious superego is as inimical to the sense of autonomy as is being driven by one's id. Freud's dictum "where Id was, there shall Ego be" (1933) should be enlarged to embrace the superego as well as the id. The enlargement of the sphere of conscious awareness of superego values and attitudes is as possible and as much to be desired as is consciousness of id impulses. Having morals, values, and ethical attitudes is all well and good as long as one knows what they are and *chooses* which ones will influence his decisions, and how.

Choices are determined—by the present situation, one's motivating feelings, and one's moral and ethical attitudes—and this is equally so if one is largely or little conscious of what those are. What consciousness provides is the possibility of checking the data, each piece with all the others, allowing reason's small voice to speak a bit louder. Conscious awareness of the data and conscious judgment checking the data become one more determinant in the complex matrix of multiple determinants involved in any given choice, and so may shift the direction of the choice. It is this that enables us to believe that we actively make our choices, and when we act without the participation of our conscious awareness and judgment we have the sense of being helplessly driven by unknown forces. It is probably true that no one may be capable of consciously knowing all of the data pertinent to a given choice, but it is the extent of that conscious awareness that determines the degree of our experience of self-mastery and ultimately affects our happiness.

AUTONOMOUS MAN

Self-mastery achieves its ultimate expression in Autonomous Man. He is a construction predicated upon the conviction that many of man's present difficulties stem from the accidents of history—that they are culturally induced and are not integral to man himself. Others have attempted such idealized portraits of what man might aspire to be, and two of these portraits—Nietzsche's Übermensch and Wilhelm Reich's Genital Character—are similar to the present sketch in several aspects. Autonomous Man, however, derives his configuration from one central and consistent attribute: He is completely open to the conscious experience of the full range of his feelings.

To Autonomous Man, no feeling is a stranger. He knows and accepts them all—his anger, shame, guilt, and greed, but also his interest, love, compassion, and joy. Because he is familiar with the full range of human passions, he does not live in fear of being surprised and overwhelmed by any feeling. Aware of the distinction between experiencing feelings and expressing feelings, he is spontaneous but not impulsive, relying upon his judgment to determine his behavioral response to feelings. He is energetic, for that is but synonymous with being open to the motivating force of feelings. He is adventurous for, knowing himself, he is relatively unafraid of external novelty. He is capable of great objectivity for, being unafraid of novelty, he has little need of the mechanism of transference distortion to create illusory familiarity. He is directed, for knowing what he feels, he knows what he wants, and he is not afraid to try to get what he wants when that appears to him to be objectively reasonable.

He is personal, open. Having accepted his own feelings, he has nothing to hide when he wishes to share, so he is capable of intimacy with others. He is empathic, for the key to any appreciation of the feelings of another is to be in touch with one's own. He is expressive—unafraid to reveal strength or gentleness, anger or love. He wants the company of others but does not consider that want a need.

He is ethical—not in slavish compliance to some externally imposed set of values and rules, but in accordance with a set of values and attitudes that he, himself, has consciously selected. He is, therefore, not constantly at war with himself. Those who are ethical through compliance to an unconsciously absorbed external dogma are frequently torn by conflict between their wishes and externally imposed rules of behavior. They must be rigidly compliant or suffer guilt for lack of compliance. Autonomous Man is flexible—since his rules are consciously his own, he may alter them as circumstance and judgment determine. He is not in conflict with himself but, instead, may be in conflict with his society, whose values and attitudes he may not wholly accept. He, therefore, tends to be political, seeking to influence social values.

He is individualistic and self-reliant. To the fullest extent possible he is master of himself and so his self-esteem is high. Although he values esteem from others he does not depend upon it, and so does not hesitate to stand up for his convictions even when they are unpopular.

He knows fear, for who can live in this world without it? But his fear is only of real danger. Most people live with far greater fear which they attribute to real dangers of the external world but which is, in actuality, largely displaced fear of themselves—fear of being overwhelmed by their own feelings. Autonomous Man, on the other hand, is not his own worst enemy.

His is the greatest chance for happiness.

Perhaps no one achieves this ideal state of autonomy, but some do approach it, and those who do are as magnets to the rest, tempting us to emulate their achievement. We admire their vitality, their self-confidence, their easy and effective execution of adaptive tasks. But must this state remain the province of a very few, or can mankind in general approach autonomy? Clearly, each of us achieves some small degree of autonomy and some few achieve a great deal. No arbitrary line of limitation can be drawn. But if progress in that direction is to be made, certain deeply ingrained mistaken notions about man and his feelings must be undone.

It must be recognized that although man is capable of

anger, hostility, greed, and excessive self-interest, these are reactive feelings, not part of the inherent disposition of man. That the tree on the mountaintop has grown twisted and stunted, deformed by harsh winds and poor soil, tells us little of the inherent nature of that tree, tells us little of how that tree might grow in better circumstances. As the human organism comes to be recognized and respected as the intensely interested, loving, and generous creature that he is, he will grow to another configuration.

8

Human Development

Cultural attitudes and expectations, deeply ingrained, play a large role in shaping mankind. But culture is not fixed and static. It is time to push back, reshaping some of those attitudes and expectations so that man may grow straighter and more true. The best place to start is with the very young who have not yet been bent out of shape.

There are two reasons to include a discussion of childhood development in a work that seeks to find our way back to feelingfulness and, thus, to autonomy and our best chance for happiness. First, it may require the passage of generations to achieve and solidify that goal, given mankind's reticence to change. But not only do we owe future generations our best effort to secure feelingful lives for them, we must also remember that we were once infants and children, too. We started out with the same innate equipment with which infants start today. A more accurate assessment of the infant than we have had, and a clearer picture of the infant's optimal development, can help to inform us of the many ways in which we may have been led astray in the course of our own development toward adulthood. So informed, we may more effectively find our own way back to feelingfulness.

THE MALIGNED INFANT

The infant and young child are probably the most misunderstood and most maligned people in the world and their only compensation for that is they are generally loved, cared for, and considered the future hope of humanity. I say that they are misunderstood and maligned because their innocent ignorance of the world and of their culture is misconstrued to reflect motives far more sophisticated than any of the child's capacities warrant. The infant is accused, and I use the term advisedly, of being narcissistic and omnipotent, which accords with the general misconception that infants are selfish and that they are bent upon controlling the world and everyone in it.

I hold that the infant is totally incapable of such concepts and attitudes, that these are adult motives projected on to the infant by adults who may love the child but who do not respect the child as fully human. Only as the child demonstrates that he has absorbed the rules of his culture is he considered to be fully human, but until then he is treated as only a potential human who must undergo a period of training to become the real thing. This misunderstanding of the infant deprives him of the respect that he needs for the development of self-esteem and autonomy, even while he is provided the loving care that assures his survival.

Some may balk at the idea that the infant is loved but not respected, yet it is easy to demonstrate. One need only cite the prevalence of scheduled feeding and of rigorous toilet training programs instituted without regard to the individuality of the child involved, or look to the popular "let 'em cry or you'll spoil 'em rotten" attitude of those who are quite convinced that to "give in" to the child is to lose the battle for dominance. The four– or five–hour feeding schedule may be based upon a statistical average, but the individual infant has no awareness of such things. If he awakes and cries at two– or three–hour intervals it is from hunger, not malice. And if his individual physiology make him feel hungry at shorter rather than longer intervals, is he simply to be trained to *feel* hungry at times that conform to some statistical norm? The child who wakes at night cries not to assert his dominance over his parents, but because he is in some way uncomfortable. Can one expect him to patiently tolerate his discomfort until morning? Try that with adults who are far better equipped! When one keeps in mind that feelings are always the psychic reflection of some disequilibrium, in the infant as in the adult, then it becomes clear that the infant's feelings are as much to be respected as the adult's.

The common idea that consideration of the child's feelings means "giving in" to the child in the battle for dominance between child and adult ascribes to the infant not only malicious intent, but also a degree of sophistication in interpersonal combat that is quite impossible in one so young. The infant starts life in an objectless world; he has not yet developed a concept of things or of people, himself or others, so to attribute any interpersonal motives at all to him is an absurdity.

Granted, the newborn infant frequently wakes and cries during the night, exhausting untold numbers of parents who, understandably, want their infants to be comfortable. Some interpret the infant's nightime cry as a demand for attention, but this cannot be. The infant exists in a world without objects and without concepts. He has no idea of the existence of parents upon whom to make demands. The infant's cry is not a demand, it is not a communication of any sort. The parent or caregiver may interpret the cry as a communication, a signal, but from the infant's side it is nothing more than a discharge action in response to some internal disequilibrium. The infant exists mostly in a state of sleep, but as he experiences disequilibrium, reflective feelings and sensations press toward arousal and action. His actions are quite limited: he may cry, suck, and thrash about; he can do nothing more. So the infant wakes and cries, not to call his parents, but in an effort to discharge the tension of some feeling or sensation in the only way available to him.

Nor is the tendency to malign the infant reserved exclusively to parents and the general public. Many of the same anachronistic motives ascribed to infants by weary caregivers have found their way into fundamental tenets of psychoanalytic theory. For example, the infant who is totally naive must of necessity exhibit a thorough lack of knowledge about the world. Yet that very unworldliness has been misinterpreted by psychologists as evidence of the infant's narcissism and omnipotence. This was a theoretical construction introduced by Freud (1914), greatly elaborated by Ferenczi (1913), and more recently re-emphasized by Kohut (1971) in his concept of a self-psychology. In this view the infant's total libido (I would prefer the term *interest*) is invested in himself from the start, accounting for his overestimation of himself as omnipotent. To protest that the infant can hardly be accused of investing libido in himself before he has developed the concept of self may seem no more than a quibble over semantics, especially since Freud's terminology specifically describes it as an investment of libido in the ego, not in the self. Still, the clear implication in Freud's article is that the infant loves only some aspect of himself and one must wonder what that means. Certainly the infant does not love others, since he has no awareness of the existence of others. If it follows that the infant is interested only in his own sensations and feelings, well then, of course! That is the totality of his experience. There is nothing more that exists for him and so there is nothing more for him to be interested in. As he matures and develops, however, experiencing more of our world in manifold ways, he will develop concepts of things and of others and of self and will be interested in all of them. No single one of these will absorb all of his interest to the exclusion of others. It is this mounting interest in everything that he experiences that Mahler (1965) and Greenacre (1960) call the infant's "growing love affair with the world." And that, at last, acknowledges the infant's capacity to love—not only himself, but the whole world of his experience.

Nor does the infant start life with a sense of omnipotence. Ferenczi (1913, p. 216f) cited the example of the infant who is apt to reach for the moon in much the way that he reaches for a ball suspended above his crib, and Ferenczi misread this as evidence of the infant's omnipotence. It is not omnipotence, but merely ignorance. If the infant knew what the moon was and where it was located, and still reached for it, that would be a very different matter. In the same way, the infant who creeps or rolls off the edge of a table or bed is not expressing some omnipotent flying fantasy. He simply does not yet know about gravity.*

Narcissism, with its self-love and omnipotent grandiosity, is not the primary condition of the infant. It is a secondary and pathological development engendered in those infants who are too frequently frustrated by their caregivers and who come to feel helpless and untrusting of the world as a result. People can be made to feel such mistrust even at a very young age. So it is no simple and inconsequential error that we make when we falsely attribute such inappropriate feelings and motives to the infant from the start, for then we cannot fully trust or respect this little being whose loveable and cuddly

---

*A related logical error in the early days of psychoanalysis made much of the similarities in magical thinking found in disturbed adults, primitive people, and children, falsely assuming that this tendency in the three groups stemmed from a common root, the primary omnipotence attributed to infancy. Children and primitive people were thought to have not yet outgrown it and disturbed adults were perceived as having regressed back to it. Apparently little thought was given to the fact that all three of those groups had already acquired some notion of causality, which the infant cannot have. To seek for explanations, even magical and omnipotent ones, once one has a concept of causality is understandable. But to assume that the infant starts life with an omnipotent belief in his own magical power to make things happen—and all this before he has developed any concept of self, of power, and of causal relationships—seems most improbable.

exterior thinly masks what we really perceive to be a selfish and tyrannical creature lurking within. Instead, we then seek to train this wild little being to conform to human dimensions and, in so doing, create the frustration and distrust that causes the infant to become what we erroneously assumed he was from the start.

Finally, we must remain mindful that as the infant is today commonly viewed, so were many of us viewed when we were infants, perhaps long years ago. Our feelings were also misunderstood and false motives mistakenly attributed to us. Regardless of whether we were loved by our parents, we were often not trusted by them, and so our parents took the measures that were conventional for that time to train such inherent evil out of us. And that was the beginning of the lesson that many of us as infants were forced to learn: that our genuine feelings were unacceptable and that, to be accepted, we had better learn to act in acceptable ways, regardless of our feelings. That has been the beginning of the road to unconscious repression of feelings for a great many people over a great many generations.

INFANT DEVELOPMENT

In psychoanalytic literature a distinction is made between maturation and development, even though both terms refer to the growth of the individual. Maturation is the term that refers to the built-in physiological mechanisms of the organism that contribute more automatically to its growth; factors that determine an infant's height and weight, the myelinization of its central nervous system permitting more refined neuromuscular function, the operation of hormone glands and timely growth of secondary sex characteristics, and so forth. Development, on the other hand, refers to those processes of growth that are more directly influenced by experience, such as the development of character and of cultural values and attitudes. The two processes are often interactive, each influencing the other to some degree, yet they remain separate processes. For the purposes of this discussion development will be our primary focus of attention and I hold that development, by its very definition, depends largely upon the human capacity to learn from the very start.

Beginnings of Communication and Mastery

Over time the infant's cry does become a signal, a form of meaningful communication. Yet this is achieved only after the infant repeatedly experiences a set of events that consistently attend his crying activity. For example, some infants as early as ten days to two weeks of age will awaken hungry and cry but then, at the sound of a mother's approaching footsteps, the cry ceases or subsides. By then a process of learning has already occured. That infant, having consistently experienced the sounds of mother's approach following upon the experience of his own crying activity, comes to associate those events along with the anticipated experiences of feeding and satiety that follow. As the infant comes to associate his cry with the events that regularly attend his crying activity, the cry takes on psychological content. Now he cries not simply to discharge tension, but also to evoke a sequence of events, and thus his cry becomes a true communication.

The infant who is consistently fed in response to his cry comes to associate those events in time, and that may well be the precise moment at which magical thinking begins for the infant. His cry brings about a desired result. The infant may not know how this happens, only that it does happen. But this moment marks not only the beginning of magical thinking, it is also the beginning of the infant's sense of mastery. For the first time the infant can now do something to effect his own state. Will this newfound sense of mastery thus turn the infant into the little tyrant that some suspected him to be all along? We know that the infant, once sated, falls back to sleep, and remains asleep until hunger or some other disequilibrium arouses him once again. We would have to attribute some inborn malice to the infant to believe that he would perversely wake and cry for no reason other than to exercise his new-found mastery.

The infant is not born angry and malicious. Frustration, pain, and helplessness may, however, cause him to become that way. Using the hunger-feeding situation as an example, we may speculate about the probable events that attend different approaches to feeding: feeding-on-demand* and feeding-on-schedule. Even as the infant sleeps his metabolism creates a disequilibrium which is reflected as a feeling of hunger. As the disequilibrium becomes greater, the feeling of hunger becomes increasingly intense, pressing toward arousal and discharge in action. The infant wakes and cries. He is helpless to restore equilibrium on his own.

If the infant is fed in response to his cry, then equilibrium is restored and he is spared the prolongation of his discomfort. Not only is this humane but also, as previously described, the associative connection between the activity of crying and feeding takes place in time, allowing the infant to feel that he has some control over his fate.

The infant fed on schedule has no such luck. He, too, wakes hungry and cries, and nothing happens until some future time when the clock determines his feeding. He will have to endure the discomfort of hunger for longer periods of time, but equally important, for him there is no consistent correlation of hunger, crying, and being fed. The feeding, when it occurs, has no connection with his own activity—the restoration of his equilibrium is arbitrary and the infant feels helpless to influence the course of events.

This is the infant who is apt to become angry, for anger is the natural response to frustration and pain. He is the one

*Note: Even this common usage—"demand feeding"—perpetuates the prejudicial view of the infant as imperious!

who is likely to *become* malicious as, at the later stage of development, he comes to realize that his pain and frustration is the result of his caretaker's actions. Then he will be prone to enter into combat with that caretaker to force compliance and, perhaps, even to exact revenge. He is the one likely to behave like a tyrant in an effort to overcome his helplessness. And, if forced far enough, he is the one who will become narcissistic (self-absorbed) and who will develop omnipotent fantasies in an effort to compensate for his feelings of impotence. Narcissism is made, not born.

Beginnings of Trust

Certainly the course of events is not so simple as this isolated example would make it seem. Much more than the hunger-feeding interaction goes on during those early days and weeks of the infant's life, and there is no intention here to suggest that the course of each person's life is irretrievably cast at that earliest time. The example is meant only to demonstrate the principle that it is excessive frustration, not indulgence, that fosters adverse development in the infant.

In psychoanalytic thought there is a belief that "optimal frustration" is most conducive to childhood development. "Optimal frustration" is that ambiguous area between not too much and not too little. The idea is that development will not proceed if there is no frustration to spur it, but that too much frustration will stunt it. I suggest that development in childhood needs no spur, will proceed if given the opportunity, and that the optimal level of frustration is simply minimal frustration. Laziness is no more an inborn characteristic of the infant than is malice or tyranny. Minimal frustration cannot be avoided, no matter how quickly the caretaker responds. There is necessarily some lapse of time between the infant's experience of hunger and the restoration of equilibrium by feeding. It is not possible to eliminate that degree of frustration—it can only be minimized. And to help minimize a child's frustration is not to overindulge the child; it is simply to respect the individual who happens also to be an infant.

When we clear away the perjorative mythology surrounding the infant what we find is simply a newborn human being. Because he is newborn he is totally naive; because he is human he is equipped with all of the capacities that we value in humans. Most of these capacities are, as yet, undeveloped. They need only develop to become clearly recognizable, and they will develop if only they are allowed. There is no need to teach the infant to think, to feel, to love, for those things, like breathing in and out, will come naturally to him.

Values are another matter. The infant is neither considerate of others, nor is he fair. Fairness, consideration of others—the very existence of others—these are social values and concepts that our very young have not yet had time to learn.

How then is it possible to ascribe a capacity for love to the infant who doesn't yet comprehend even the existence of others to love? When one understands that love is interest—the most intense form of interest—then the answer becomes clear. The infant is from the very start interested, at times intensely so, in all manner of things that comprise his world. The fact that people do not yet inhabit his world, and the very concept of others remains foreign to him, means only that his interest in these early days must be directed elsewhere.

Referring once again to Alexander's theory of Surplus Energy, we understand that the entirety of the newborn infant's energy is first directed to the establishment and maintenance of equilibrium—respiration, heat regulation, digestion and evacuation, and so on. In a matter of days, perhaps a week or two, however, a degree of equilibrium is established and now there is excess energy (libido or, preferably, interest) that can be directed toward a wider range of events.

At first the infant existed almost entirely in a state of sleep, aroused only periodically by the reflective feelings of internal disequilibrium pressing toward discharge in action. Now the infant begins to have periods of wakefulness of another sort. It is a quiet wakefulness in which the infant may make cooing sounds and show some gentle random movement, but the intense discharge activities of crying and thrashing about have ceased. Now the infant is attending to the stimuli that impinge upon him—the sounds and sights and the tactile sensations that comprise his world. I take this focused attention to be an expression of interest, and as the establishment of equilibrium proceeds the increase in available excess energy is expressed in an expanding interest and directed attention. The infant is interested in his world and is learning about it.

The infant's total experience, at this stage, consists of sensations and feelings, and that's where his interest and attention go. Objects and the notion of causality are concepts that have not yet developed and cannot be attributed to the infant. Even *mother* (taken here as shorthand for primary caregiver) is not an object, though we as observers know that the infant's existence is dependent upon her care. To the infant, mother is only an associated group of sensations and feelings—visual, olfactory, auditory, tactile, and kinesthetic sensations as well as hunger and satiety feelings—experienced by the infant as pleasurable or painful, depending upon their intensities.

In the hunger-feeding situation this set of sensations and feelings is experienced in simultaneity or in a particular sequence. As previously discussed, the repetition of this set of sensations and feelings becomes associatively connected for the infant so that as early as ten days to two weeks some infants, on waking hungry, will respond to the approach of a mother's footsteps with a cessation or diminution of their cry. The quieting down of the infant, even before his hunger is sated, is evidence of how the infant can now anticipate the learned sequence of sensations and feelings eventuating in feeding and satiety. If the feeding experience is consistently satisfying, then the infant will develop the beginnings of an attitude which has been variously described as optimism (Erikson, 1950), hope (French, 1952), or confidence (Benedek, 1967). Conversely, if that experience is consistently frustrating and is repeatedly felt to be painful or unpleasurable, then the opposite attitude will begin to be established. This is not to say that the attitude of optimism or pessimism is at this point indelibly stamped upon the infant. The infant's attitude and outlook will, of course, be subject to change by subsequent experiences, yet those earliest experiences are very significant in establishing an attitudinal tone.

Since the experience of sequences of sensations and feelings is the only measure of the world the infant knows, the question of whether these are, on balance, pleasurable or unpleasurable is of profound consequence indeed. Not only will the degree of pleasure or unpleasure in these early days set the tone for an attitude of optimism, hope, or trust, but this will also set the scene for an appraisal of the worth of the infant's very existence. It is premature to speak of self-esteem in the infant since the concept of self will only develop at a later time. Still, it is hard to imagine that the balance between the pleasure and unpleasure of his existence will not play an important role in determining his later appraisal of self-worth.

THE TODDLER

Beginnings of Individuation

At the toddler stage of development, the young child is no longer the totally naive and uninformed infant he once was. Through maturation and development he has come to establish boundaries between self and not-self, and come to recognize objects and persons at least in a rudimentary way. The toddler has developed some notion of causality, even though that may be largely magical in content. Is this more worldly-

wise creature still to be trusted or will he now use his knowledge and power to abuse those upon whom he still depends?
If he has been excessively frustrated in the past, then he will
very likely engage in a battle of wills as a matter of course, but
if he has not been angered by earlier mistreatment there is no
reason to assume that the child's innate loving nature will
change except, perhaps, to become more evident and more
focused.

At this point in development the child clearly recognizes
mother as a person upon whom, from the observer's point of
view, he is still almost totally dependent. I qualify that, for it
is not clear that the child, himself, recognizes his dependency.
After all, when he feels hungry and cries, his mother feeds
him. Or when he is wet and cold and calls for aid, mother
makes him comfortable. To him it must seem that he exerts
some control over his own situation. But perhaps the discussion of his own recognition of his dependency is beside the
point. What is most relevant is that he does not feel helpless
though he is, in fact, dependent upon her care. As he is able to
get mother to respond to his cues, so he feels to some degree
in control of his fate. But as mother fails to respond appropriately, he does feel helpless and unable to control his own
conditions through her ministrations.

This particular stage of interaction between young child
and mother is one that touches upon many key issues. For
one, what transpires here has a direct effect upon the young
child's emerging self-esteeming function. As he is confronted
with his helplessness consequent to the mother's lack of appropriate response to his needs, so his self-esteem will be
lowered. One could argue that the child is wrong to devalue
himself for his mother's lack of responsiveness—that he
should devalue her instead. Perhaps this is true, but the young
child lacks the clear objectivity and rationality that would
enable him to find fault with his mother. He will probably be
angry with the withholding mother, but it is the child himself

that feels helpless, unable to evoke his mother's appropriate response, and his self-esteem will be correspondingly low.

Responsive ministration continues to be the way to foster high self-esteem and generosity in the child. There is good evidence that the demanding, clinging, and tyrannical child is the one who has been forced into that position by a frustrating, unresponsive, or inappropriately responsive caretaker. Many of the difficulties in loving find their roots in the frustrating experiences of childhood.

An interesting situation, easily observable, bears directly on the matter. Picture a mother occupied with reading or knitting or absorbed in some other quiet activity, with her toddler (about eighteen months) on the floor beside her chair, playing with his own toys. If one observes a number of such situations one finds a good deal of variation in the childrens' behavior. Some children will stay right at mother's side, some will wander a few feet away and then return, and others, periodically looking back to check on mother, will even venture into an adjoining room where visual contact with the mother is broken.

Does the child who stays at mother's side love her more than does the child who explores his environment? The prevalent psychoanalytic view is that the exploring child is one who has internalized a good mother—he takes her with him as he goes, so to speak—while the one who sticks to mother has failed to do so. But the psychoanalytic term *internalization*, (like the related terms *incorporation, introjection,* and *identification,*) have been so variously and ambiguously employed in the professional literature that I prefer more directly descriptive language. It is enough to say that the child who explores is the one who *trusts* his mother. He has learned through experience that his mother is reliable and dependable—that she will be there for him when and if he needs her. Conversely, the child who clings to mother, sticks by her side, does not love her more but trusts her less.

It is the untrusting child who is clinging and demanding

and who may become whimsical and manipulative in his effort to test the mother to convince himself finally of her reliability. He was not born that way but was led there by his negative experience.

This situation graphically portrays the failure to develop an adequate sense of separateness and demonstrates how excessive dependency is fostered in the child. It is not the result of overindulgence, of "spoiling," as so many are prone to believe. The young child is still quite helpless and he will, from time to time, encounter internal or external events that cause him discomfort that he cannot resolve on his own. He needs a caretaker who will intervene on his behalf. It stands to reason that the child who feels secure in that benevolent intervention will tend to venture more. He will be less fearful of his interest in his world, for he knows that if he encounters discomfort he will soon be rescued. So he explores a wider world, and in the course of that exploration accumulates experience of his own coping capacities. His dependable "back-up" allows him greater knowledge of his world and of his self, contributing to his greater self reliance.

The child lacking dependable "back-up" is fearful of encountering discomfort, not knowing when or if he will be rescued. He tends to constrict his world, to "play it safe," and he accumulates less experience of his world and of his self, thereby perpetuating his need of a caretaker. Prolonged and excessive dependency is the product of fear.

All young children are, of course, dependant, but when a given child fails to effect an adequate sense of seperateness then his dependancy becomes intensified and is marked by possessiveness. One often hears a proud mother exclaim that her clinging child loves her so much that he won't allow her out of his sight. But as we have seen, that is probably more distrust than love, and so the element of possessiveness enters into some relationships at a very early stage of development. If one cannot rely upon a desired person or object to be there when one wants or needs it, then one way to try to dispel the resulting uncertainty is to possess it, to try to make it part of one's self and thereby completely control it. Although the untrusting child is also a loving child, often the excessive dependency and possessiveness become confused with love by the attending adults, just as dependency and love are apt to be confused later in the child's mind.

Conversely, the child who develops greater trust and a sense of seperateness can tolerate the mother's absence more, but he loves her no less. He will often *want* to be with mother while the less individuated child will believe that he *needs* to be with mother. The former child is on his way toward the development of a generous love, but the love of the needy child is already encumbered by anger, distrust, and possessiveness, and if this direction remains unchanged by subsequent experience he will love only cautiously, demanding first to be loved as a guarantee in advance that his neediness will be satisfied.

THE WALKING-TALKING CHILD

The principle of minimal frustration being the optimal spur to a child's development holds beyond infancy, and applies just as firmly to the child as he grows older and more mature, even though, admittedly, the child's acquisition of motility, experience, and some degree of knowledge will make the situation more complex. The child's expanding interest in the world, manifested as intense curiosity about all manner of things, combined with a newfound motility, may lead the child into any number of potentially dangerous situations. Some frustration is imperative when a child wishes to explore electrical connections or to investigate an open third floor window. Obviously the child must be stopped but that frustration is in the service of his physical safety. Here the tact and empathy of the caretaker is put to the test, for the caretaker must intervene in a way that makes it clear to the child that it is that particular situation that is prohibited, not the feeling of interest and curiosity. The caretaker who sees potential danger everywhere and who reacts with excessive anxiety to any attempt of the child to venture will convey to the child a prohibition against the feeling of interest and curiosity. Such a prohibition against feeling is far more frustrating to the child than is the physical removal from a particular situation.

Is the child, then, to be permitted his own way in all things short of real physical danger? Certainly! That is how the child learns about his world and about his own capacity to cope with it. And the caretaker must be at hand to help the child if he needs help or to rescue him if that is required. It can be an exhausting task for the caretaker, as any number of mothers will attest. And sometimes a limit must be set based on that person's endurance rather than on the child's optimal development. Mother, too, is a person and is entitled to consideration from the rest of us even if not from the child, who does not yet understand such limitations. But when such justified limitations are set, let them rest on their own merits. They need not be exercised or rationalized away as being in the child's best interests, citing the mythic dangers of permissiveness or of overindulgence.

Permissiveness refers only to a willingness to allow the child's capacities to evolve without obstruction, and indulgence refers to the humane and appropriate response to the child. But a note of caution is in order. Permissiveness without adequate back-up support is simply neglect. And indulgence becomes the "overindulgence" that "spoils" the child when the child is given too much of that which is not important to him while he is being deprived of those things that are his legitimate wants and needs.

The practice of toilet training remains a persistent affront to the young child, presumably based on the notion held by some adults that children enjoy living in soiled diapers and will continue to do so if permitted. Observation quickly disproves that thesis. Children uniformly complain about cold, wet diapers, clearly indicating their discomfort, and none would freely choose that option. But sphincter control is a matter, first, of neuromuscular development, which occurs at varying times in different individuals. Secondly, the child must learn that there is an alternative option, that there is such a thing as a toilet designed for that use. Given that awareness, and the necessary sphincter control, every child will opt for the use of the toilet unless that matter has become a battleground over the issue of who is going to control that child's body—the parent or the child, himself.

"Toilet teaching" is in order when the child is old enough to comprehend its meaning, and he will usually indicate his readiness by showing his curiosity about the toilet and its use by adults. "Toilet training," which usually consists of placing the child on the toilet at set times for set periods with an expectation that he urinate or defecate on demand, is not in order, for it deprives the child of the opportunity to control his own bodily functions and reemphasizes his feeling of helplessness.

What is to be emphasized here is the child's capacity to learn and his eagerness to do so, if given half a chance. It is fascinating and mysterious to listen to proud parents and grandparents who, in one breath, describe the billiance of a young child and then, in the next, reveal that they hold some archane belief in the child's stubborn clinging to a primitive and uncomfortable way of life. The child does not cling stubbornly to ignorance, but learning takes time and patient support. And when it is demanded of the child that he learn a particular step in acculturation before he is physically, emotionally, and intellectually ready to make that step, then he is forced to feel helpless and inadequate and he will most probably become angry and rebellious. The child does not start out stubborn, but when pushed too hard too early he will become stubborn, and then adult misconceptions become self-fulfilling prophecies.

Learning and Education

The education of children has become a focus of interest and of intense debate within our society. Daycare, preschools, and head start programs have become increasingly popular and matriculation in junior kindergartens of "good" schools has become as expensive and as difficult as starting college used to be not all that many years ago. There are numerous complex social issues involved in this scramble for early education of children that require careful sorting out, but there are certain fundamental facts that tend to be ignored or overlooked. The education of children does not begin when they enter schools of any kind—it begins in the earliest days of infancy. And schooling, whenever it begins, should not be considered as something separate from the overall development of the child.

Look at the achievements of the child during his first four or five years of life. He has developed boundaries between self and not-self, he has achieved language and motility, he has developed the concept of causality and has absorbed many of the values of his culture. Simple maturation, by which I mean physiological growth, plays a part in some of those achievements, but learning also plays a major role. Indeed, the first four or five years constitute the most intensive learning period in every person's life.

Parents everywhere will attest to the fact that young children, once they have acquired language, are constantly questioning everything from "Why is the sky blue?" to "Where do babies come from?" In the early days of psychoanalysis the prevalent thought held that the child's constant questioning of everything was simply a displacement from his central question about the mysteries of sex, about which he was unable to be direct. Perhaps that sexual bias derived from the sexually repressive atmosphere in middle Europe during the late nineteenth century, as well as from the then revolutionary discovery that even very young children were sexual beings. There is little reason to continue that bias now. Of course children are curious about sexual matters, but they are also curious about every aspect of the world in which they live, and the basis of that curiosity is not simply a displacement from sex but is a striving for mastery in order to overcome feelings of help-lessness.

Young children are intense students who will be busily engaged in learning, whether or not they are in school, for the whole world of their experience is their primary classroom. They may learn different things in school than at home alone with mother or father, but then it becomes a matter of deter-mining what is important for them to learn and under which circumstances they are most apt to learn profitably.

Most full-time mothers are quite convinced that being home alone with their two-year-old child is a full-time oc-cupation. Imagine, then, the demand upon the daycare per-son or preschool teacher who, under the most enlightened circumstances, must attend six or eight or ten such children. Such a person must be endowed with prodigious vitality and interest to keep up with a whole brood, or else the children are not getting the same individual care and attention that they would receive in a one-on-one situation.

Unfortunately we do not live in an ideal world and for increasing numbers of us the debate over what situation would afford our children the optimal benefits is simply not a luxury in which we can afford to indulge. Today, many fam-ilies require two incomes; both husband and wife have to share the financial burdens if the family is to survive. There is also a sharp increase in the number of single parent families where it is imperative that the parent work to provide for their family. To this is added the disappearance of the extended family which means that there may be no grandparents, aunts, or uncles to look after the children when parents are at work. (It is all too clear that daycare facilities and preschools are very much a necessity in today's world.) Ultimately, what is a practical necessity for us and what is an optimal situation for our children are not necessarily one and the same.

On the other extreme, in families where cost is no object, more and more parents are opting to send their children to schools, play groups, and classes of various kinds at younger and younger ages. These are parents who have been led to believe, or to rationalize, that they are sending their children off to spend hours in such programs for the good of the child. In our competitive society it is commonly believed that early education is preparation for success, a way of giving the child a head start toward future achievement. Yet for the sake of a future tomorrow we too often overlook what we are asking of our children today: in this case, to trust and to depend upon strangers before he has fully learned to trust and to depend upon his own mother and father. The child placed in a school setting is expected, moreover, to share with other children, wait his turn, be considerate of others—and all this before the child himself has any feeling to incline himself in those directions. Certainly, if the coercion is sufficient, the child can be trained in these socially acceptable ways, but then he is acting out of concert with his own feelings and without any real comprehension of his behavior. The child will feel like sharing, if given sufficient time and support, but he cannot be prematurely trained to *feel* like sharing; he cannot be trained to *feel* any particular feeling, except perhaps fear and helplessness, which often attend excessive coercion. Such training often divorces action from feeling and sets the stage for the development of chronic boredom.

What then of the parents who point with pride to their school-ified child who by the age of two has learned to recite the alphabet or to tie his own shoelaces? There is no evidence that learning the alphabet early in any way contributes to a later interest in reading, or that tying one's shoelaces by two contributes to later proficiency in engineering or in fashion design. I would remind them of a much-ignored fact: it was the children of the baby boom in the mid and late forties who were the first to be subject to the wide popularization of early education and those were the same children who, in the late sixties, provided us with the highest college dropout rate in our history. Other social factors may have played a role in that, but the stage was set by the premature socialization of those boom-babies of the forties (Bernstein, 1975).

The mere accumulation of information by children is inevitable, whether they are in a formal setting or not. Some will learn faster than others, depending on innate capacity and opportunity, but essential to the child's learning is his wish to know and his courage to try. His wish to know, his curiosity, is simply a measure of his interest in his world, and that will continue unless it is cut off by excessive frustration. His courage to try is a measure of his emerging self-esteem and those with high self-esteem are more willing to try for they are less afraid of possible failure.

The home setting with its one-on-one relationship with a parent is far more conducive to the child's expanding interest and evolving self-esteem than is the school setting with its demands of premature socialization. And if the school setting does provide a wider opportunity for the accumulation of information, that is not as important a matter at this juncture. The unobstructed interest and the higher self-esteem of the child who spent those early years at home will allow him to easily catch up with the accumulated knowledge of the early schooled child, and will better equip him for the school years ahead.

But schooling must begin at some point. It is better to begin at age four or five than at age two, for the four- or five-year-old is far better equipped to cope with the social situation and the discipline demands of the school experience. He has learned, by then, techniques for managing the tension of his feelings far better than has the two- or three-year-old child. Even at four or five, however, the maintenance of interest and the fostering of self-esteem remain central to his development and education.

The talented teacher of young children understands that they are individuals who are ready to learn different things at different times, depending upon their variable maturation and development, as well as upon their differing life experiences and the particular interests thereby engendered. Unless this individuality is recognized by the teacher as well as by the parents, the imposition of lock-step education may accomplish compliance but at the cost of loss of the child's interest in learning. And when the child loses his interest in learning, then he will be bored by school and will appear to be lazy and easily distracted. How many children branded "learning disabled" are really children who have been turned off by excessive frustration? That would be a worthy study in its own right.

The tendency toward uniformity in our formal educational system disregards individual differences, treating all children as though they should be interested in the same things at the same time. The stress on efficiency creates a systematic emphasis on teaching rather than on learning (teaching is what the teacher does, learning is what the children do). This, combined with parental ambition—wishing their child to do well—places great pressure on the child to conform, to learn what he is taught rather than to learn what he is interested in learning at any particular time. In these early school years the child with good self-esteem is likely to rebel against such treatment, either directly and verbally, or indirectly by being naughty, unruly. Those with lower self-esteem will be more easily cowed and will conform, sometimes becoming overachievers in their bid to win esteem from others.

Some teachers have the talent and sensitivity to understand young children and intuitively know that the preeminent task of early education is the maintenance and fostering of self-esteem. They listen to children, respecting their interests, their ideas, and their questions. But many teachers lack that talent or soon lose patience under the pressure of large class size and the need to demonstrate so-called achievement as measured by various standardized tests. Parents must realize that these early school years are not merely education, they are a crucial part of the child's development. Just as war is too important an issue to be left to the military, so early education is too important to be left to the educators. Parents must actively participate in the school experience and, beyond that, must realize that the child's education is still the parents' responsibility. A parent may or may not be able to influence a particular teacher or a local school system, but they can have a very direct effect upon the child as soon as they recognize that his education does not start and stop with the school day. The child is interested and is learning all of the time, and the parent who will respond to the child's wish to know will do much to alleviate the tedium of a too rigidly structured classroom during the school day.

The growing emphasis on achievement is often detrimental, especially when used in combination with the social need of working parents as a justification for placing children in daycare centers and preschools at the age of two or three. This is supposed to give children a head start in education but it actually demands a premature acculturation, placing constraints on them that they are not yet ready to understand and absorb. The resultant deleterious effects far outweigh any theoretical educational advantage that is anticipated. And how does one identify and measure achievement in these early years? There are no standardized tests for trust, self-confidence, self-esteem. When important things defy easy and precise measurement, there is a tendency to turn to those things that can be measured and to make them the sole criteria of achievement, whether they are significant or not. So memorizing numbers and letters and colors becomes the measurable "achievement," as though that were what really mattered at this young age.

The mere accumulation of information is inevitable and it matters little if the child learns the alphabet at age two or age six. The child's later interest in reading does not depend upon memorizing the alphabet early; it depends far more upon the maintenance of his interest in general and the value placed upon the activity of reading. Many parents who complain that the school has failed to "teach their children to be interested in reading" are people who have few or no books in the home and have little or no interest in reading themselves. School is only an adjunct to the child's education and parents must learn to view it that way.

Learning Self-Discipline

One question so often addressed to me that it must reflect a central concern is, "If the young child is not disciplined, how will he ever learn discipline?" What appears here as a rather straight forward question really involves a whole complex of issues. Accepting self-discipline as a positive value (it is an expression of self-mastery), the question above clearly implies a notion that self-discipline is acquired through the imposition of external discipline. I see no evidence for that. Imposed discipline, if sufficiently rigorous, may create compliance, and perhaps that is the real implicit goal. Then those parents believe that the "child with discipline" is the child who compliantly accepts the parents' discipline. Compliance is confused with being disciplined.

Furthermore, the question implies that the child has a native distaste for order and efficiency. Yet what looks to us like a preference for the unregulated life is only the young child's inability to anticipate future events. He leaves his playthings strewn about not because he imperiously expects his parents to keep things in order for him, but because he does not yet have the capacity to think about tomorrow. He cannot anticipate the future, and his future wishes; all that exists for him is now. And that also explains why his tolerance of frustration is so low. He cannot think in terms of future gratification, or of alleviation of some present discomfort at some near future time. All that exists for him is the present, and the present has no end.

With patient support the child will develop a sense of time, a concept of future, and as he does so, his tolerance of frustration will grow as will his capacity to anticipate his future wishes. As he develops a concept of future time he will order his life accordingly, but the demand that he order his future before "future" exists for him is to insist that he compromise the "now," which is all that has meaning for him.

Learning to Be Independent

In the earlier section on the development of the toddler we reviewed the process of individuation by which the toddler begins to develop a sense of his own seperateness, a necessary step on the way toward independence. But it is only a necessary first step. He continues to be very dependent, for he is almost totally unable to satisfy his own wants and needs and must depend upon his caretakers for their help. Although this dependency is generally deemed acceptable by adults at first, there is a pervasive suspicion that it will become a habit if allowed to continue, a belief that the child must be taught to be independent. Nothing could be farther from the truth. The child must learn that he can be *dependent*, that he can trust the back-up support of his caretakers, and as that is established his independence will proceed quite automatically.

No child wishes to be helplessly dependent unless forced to the conclusion that efforts toward achieving independence are fraught with too much danger and discomfort. The parent who can tolerate the messiness of it will find that the child will attempt to feed himself at a very young age. As soon as he is physically able, the child will creep, then crawl, then stand

and walk. As soon as he establishes motility, the child will begin to venture, to explore. These are all early attempts at independence, and they will expand as the child's capacities expand. It takes great effort to hold the child back, to keep him dependent, but that can be, and often is, accomplished.

Adults must become more precise about their expectations of young children. Parents usually want their children to achieve some degree of independence, but at the same time they want their children to be well-behaved and well-mannered. Often those two wishes come into direct conflict with each other, especially when parents press their children toward too early acculturation. The demand that children behave in socially acceptable ways before they can understand the purpose and significance of such behavior requires compliance that is antithetical to independence.

What adults really want is the cooperation of their children, and children can be and will be cooperative if allowed to be so. Their loving feelings toward parents make them want to please. But cooperation requires mutuality; it is not compliant submission of one individual to another. Overzealous pressure toward compliance bespeaks the parents' lack of trust. It is an effort to force the issue early, exploiting the young child's dependence and vulnerability, instead of relying on the child's good will and evolving reason. The effort to force compliance will meet with resistance, for even the young child will fight for integrity.

Integrity is clearly not a conceptualized principle at this age, but there is within each human being a very strong impulse and desire to be one's own person. Our feelings are the core of our being, and they are what matter, what give us substance. As we are constructed, our actions are primarily determined by our feelings, and when we act without feeling we are like automatons. It is our inherent tendency to act on feeling but, in time, we allow reason and judgment to intervene, to modulate and influence our actions. When we do allow reason and judgment to intervene, it is because we have come to have some feeling about using reason and judgment—our own reason, our own judgment.

The child must be allowed to develop his reason and his judgment, and must be allowed to develop some feeling about their use, before he can be expected to use them. When the child is forced to comply with parental demands too early, he is forced to ignore his own feelings and accept his parents' demands as the determinant of his actions. If this coercion is persistent and pervasive, the child will be torn between his own feelings and parental demands. Either he will be rebellious and angry or, if the threat of punishment and abandonment is sufficient, he will resolve the conflict by repressing his own feelings. Then he will be a compliant "clue-seeker," a person who has lost touch with his internal cues to action—his feelings—and who therefore looks always to some outside source to determine his actions. His will be a conformist existence, devoid of interest and vitality, and he will suffer chronic boredom.

The child who can trust the back-up support of his parents will feel free to venture. Having the help of those caretakers, he does not feel helpless, and so his interest in novelty will not be hedged around with excessive fear of consequences. His knowledge is still not wide and his judgment is not yet mature, so his caretakers must set limits for him. But the more he is able to venture, the more knowledge of our world will accrue to him. It is that experience, plus parental teaching, that will foster the expansion of his adaptive capacities. This developing sense of mastery over himself in relation to the world will reinforce his natural tendency toward independence. Parental respect for his feelings—taking those feelings seriously and regarding them as fully valid and human—will enable him to continue to be in full communication with his feelings, enhancing his self-esteem and enabling him to maintain his native vitality.

Learning to Love

Loving is not learned. As we have seen, the infant is interested and loving from the start. When we speak of the child's developing capacity to love, we must be very clear that we are not talking about the development of his loving *feelings*, but we are talking about the evolution of many attendant aspects of his *behavior* that are determined by his ignorance and his innocence; behaviors that obscure the adults' view of the child's love. An example, previously described, is the early infant's apparent preoccupation with what goes on within himself. The attending adult, viewing this behavior in adult terms, sees this as the infant's total self involvement and concludes that the infant loves no one but himself. The adult does not really understand that other people do not yet exist in the infant mentality. Were another adult to behave in a similarly self involved way, we might quite correctly demean that person for taking no cognizance of other people, for we do expect grown people to have a concept of others. Totally self involved behavior in the adult may well be an expression of narcissism, but in the infant it is not narcissism, it is simply an appropriate expression of the child's natural limitation at that age.

As the infant matures and develops into a young child, his love *begins* to become more discernible to the observing adult. This happens not because the child's loving feelings have changed, but because his increased knowledge, his awareness of the existence of others, even his maturing neuromuscular coordination, allow him now to behave in ways that are more recognizeable as loving in the eyes of the adult. The three— or six-month-old infant, being fed in his highchair, scoops food from his dish with his hand and offers it to mother. When we pause to consider this behavior, we have to recognize that it represents a great gesture of love. Still, it is often treated as a cute little bit of mimickry, and dismissed.

The child does not yet know about sending roses! He gives what is valued by him, and he gives it generously and lovingly. That the gesture may be imitative is quite beside the point. Of course he learns a great deal by imitation at this age, but it is the feeling that prompts the action that is important. And so it is with the two- to three-year-old who clumsily attempts to help mother with the housework, or the kindergarten child who brings her his first paper cut-out or drawing.

The child who clings to the parent with a strong embrace is not only clinging; there is much love in that embrace, as well, but the clarity of his dependency tends to cloud our view of the love that is also there. And the four- or five-year-old who speaks of marrying mommy or daddy is not just play-acting; he is speaking his love. So even when the child's behavior becomes more clearly loving it is not quite believed, perhaps because adults maintain the prejudicial view that little people can have only little feelings.

Psychoanalysts, at least, recognize the intensity and sincerity of the love of the parent by the child who has reached the oedipal level of development; around the age of four to six years. Although they have made little note of the child's love for parents before that age, presumably they do not assume that the strong love of the oedipal child arises *de novo* at the age of four or five. That love has been there all along; it simply becomes more directed and more manifest at that age and stage of development.

As the child matures and develops, his "growing love affair with the world" will become ever more clearly discernible as long as the disabling experiences of childhood do not create too much fear and distrust within him. Recognition of his love is a significant issue. If it goes unrecognized, he feels that *he* is unrecognized, and if it is dismissed as a cute little bit of imitation, then he feels trivialized. But as his love is recognized and taken seriously, he feels that his love is valued and that, therefore, he has something of value to offer. And then, being unafraid to experience his feelings, he will continue to be generously interested and loving.

THE ROLE OF PARENTAL LOVE

Perhaps this is the place to examine the child's need to be loved. It is quite widely accepted that it is very important to the child's development that he feel loved by his parents, and with this sentiment I have no quarrel. However, I do object to that unadorned statement when it leads some to the conclusion that parental love has a mysterious and magical quality that instills in the child a feeling of self-worth. Love has no such magic, and many dearly loved children grow to have low self-esteem.

What is important to the child in the development of his self-esteem is the parents' respect. Children are far more often loved than they are respected. They are loved as cute little playthings, or as extensions of the parent, or even as potential human beings who will be entitled to respect at some later time when they achieve full human status. Not often enough are they respected as fully human from the start, with genuine feelings that deserve to be recognized and appreciated as any human's feelings should be.

A clear demonstration that love alone does not contribute to a child's self-esteem is the example of the narcissistic mother who most dearly loves her child, but sees the child only as an extension or image of herself. For her, the capacity for empathy is severely damaged for she sees and hears only what she, herself, is feeling. Her responses to her child are always in terms of her own feelings and she does not truly know or understand what the child is feeling. As real and intense as her love toward the child may be, her inability to respect the child's individuality and to respond to what the child is feeling leaves the child feeling helpless and lowers his self-esteem.

It is important to understand how parental love *and* respect join in contributing to the child's optimal development. First, the parent must know what the child is feeling if he is to understand what the child wants or needs. That capacity to know and understand another's feelings is empathy. But knowing is not enough. One has also to act, to be responsive to those needs, if the child's discomfort and frustration are to be minimized, and that requires respect for the child's feelings. This is precisely where the mother's love of the child becomes a most significant factor. The mother who truly loves (is intensely interested in) her child, who has made that child another focus of her being, gives attention to that child effortlessly. That attention enhances the mother's empathy and facilitates her responsiveness. Without love (intense interest in), the effort of paying attention to the child becomes much greater and leads more rapidly to exhaustion. So it is parental empathy and respectful responsiveness that fosters the child's self-esteem: and it is parental love that enhances parental empathy and responsiveness.

The failure of parents to respect the child, to respect his needs and wants, creates for him an ambience of frustration and discomfort and a conviction of helplessness in exercising any control over his own state. The balance of unpleasure of his existence and his helplessness to correct that balance lowers his self-esteem. His inability to trust and to depend upon his caretakers limits his ability to venture, to explore himself and his world and, thereby, to expand his autonomy. He becomes clinging and dependent instead. For him, feelings become ringed around with fear; even love becomes fraught with the danger of rejection. His dependency elevates acceptance to primary importance and his low self-esteem makes him doubt his acceptability. The more he doubts his acceptability, the more difficult intimacy becomes. His love becomes possessive, not generous, and he will seek to be loved as a guarantee up front before he will even venture to be loving. This will especially be so if his early expressions of love were dimissed as trivial, for then love will be not only dangerous but humiliating, as well. And as he grows, his conscious or unconscious awareness of his inability to love, to be interested in things and in people, is sensed as a serious impairment of his own function, which further lowers his self-esteem.

Those who are raised by respectful, as well as loving, parents are fortunate, for they are apt to be feelingful people throughout their lives. Happiness is most achievable for them.

THE PRE-ADOLESCENT AND THE ADOLESCENT

As the child grows older he becomes increasingly independent, and the more independent the child becomes, the more he experiences the confusing mixed messages of parental conflict. Parents want him to be independent, responsible, self-sufficient, but they also want him to be safe and they want to be spared the uncertainty and fear that his independent behavior creates for them. They do not entirely trust the pre-adolescent's judgment, and in this they are quite correct. The pre-adolescent, and the adolescent, still have much to learn—their level of sophistication is not very high. Then when can one begin to trust their judgment, at the magical age of twenty-one? They will know more at thirty, their judgment will probably be even better at forty. But they are not going to wait. They are working at a new adaptive task, attempting the transition from child to adult, and they can acquire this new social role only through experience. Just as no one becomes an accomplished equestrian without a fair share of bumps, bruises, and sore muscles accrued in the beginner's process of learning, so the pre-adolescent and the adolescent will take their share of falls. They have to begin the process at some point and they will indicate quite clearly their readiness. Once again, the dependable back-up support of parents is required at this time, to soften the blows and to prevent excessive risks.

Most people do not realize that the pre-adolescent and adolescent are at least as scared of the novelty of this transition as are the parents. If the child has been taught to be excessively ashamed of his fear, then he will try to hide his fear behind a facade of bravado, attempting to act too grown-up too fast. The child who has been treated with respect, however, will feel that he has nothing to hide, and he will communicate his fears and seek his parents' council. It is the excessively dependent child who thinks he must act very independently, while the more truly independent child is not ashamed or afraid to admit his realistic continued dependency.

The pre-adolescent and the adolescent, like the toddler, are exploring a new world of experience. But this time it's a new world of social roles, a matter of learning to accept greater responsibility, of learning sexual competence and comfort with those of opposite gender. They are like toddlers in the grown-up world, and they require the same degree of respect and of trust in their humanness that the real toddler requires in his world. Given this, and reliable support, they will become comfortable and successful adults, well on their way to autonomy. They should not be hurried, they should not be held back; they should be allowed to evolve.

ADULT DEVELOPMENT

Adult's misconceptions about the nature of infants and children derive from their own self-perceptions. They recognize within themselves excessive anger, rebellion against authority, tendencies toward tyranny, and wishes for omnipotence, as well as reservations about loving and fear of intimacy. Not knowing or recognizing the childhood experiences and influences that caused them to become the way they are, they understandably assume that they are that way because it is the nature of humans to be that way. And from there it's an easy step to assume that the child is that way from the start.

Too often this prejudiced view of human nature is accepted as fixed and given, leading many to the cynical conclusion that attempts at change are futile and that the goal of happiness is illusory, impossible to achieve. They declare unhappiness and discontent to be the "condition of man" and, in doing so, they foreclose on the possibility of a fuller, livelier life. Some of them seem to have given up and create the forlorn impression that they are simply living out their lives with no other goal than to wait for the end to come. That is a waste.

Change is possible. How many of you have not had the experience of your life being significantly changed by spending a semester with a wise and understanding fourth grade teacher, or an equally wise professor during your junior year in college? How many have had their lives turned around by a felicitous encounter with a good friend, a sweetheart, a spouse? If you have not had that fortunate experience, yourself, then certainly you have heard, at least, similar stories from the lives of others. Far more often than we realize we are unwitting "therapists" to each other. And when one carefully analyzes those stories, one usually finds that the thing that made the difference was the respectful recognition and acceptance of some feeling or set of feelings by some respected person.

Human development is not restricted to the infant and child; it is an ongoing process that need not stop at some fixed or certain age. The adult, too, may continue his development toward autonomy, but his will be a more tortuous way for he has already taken many wrong turns and will have to find his way back to feelingfulness. To do so, he or she must be willing to entertain the notion that change is possible and that feelings cannot be judged right or wrong, good or evil, but only human. It is the proper province of society to judge our *actions,* so each person is responsible for the use of his in-

Human Development

formed judgement to decide how he or she shall *act* upon his or her feelings, and that requires that a clear distinction be made between feeling and action.

Some will seek their own way back to feelingfulness; the more adventurous will seek psychoanalytic help to find their way. Those who seek their own way can succeed, but they leave much to chance, for who can be sure that they will encounter the mentor or friend, or perhaps even the proper lonely circumstance, that will sufficiently encourage them to bring their feelings into clearer conscious awareness? Too often the force of society's values encourage people to try to hide some of their feelings by pushing them into some dark corner of the mind where the unconscious and automatic exclusionary process of repression exerts its influence. Psychoanalytic treatment, on the other hand, is specifically designed to counter repression, to restore one's feelings to one's self, to enable one to achieve greater self-mastery. It is not always an easy route, but it is the most direct one.

9
Psychoanalysis: Method and Goal

Psychoanalysis is a process of self-familiarization. So simple a description is not meant to make the task sound easy, but to lift some of the veil of mystery that seems to cloud people's perception of it. Finding one's way back to feelingfulness is never easy, but those who choose the route of psychoanalytic treatment often find it to be a most rewarding journey.

From its beginning, psychoanalysis has placed a great deal of emphasis upon "the unconscious" and has directed its attention to the undoing of repressions. Employing the technique of free association and the engendered transference distortions that arise, it seeks to uncover repressed significant historical events in the individual's life. However, the recovery of personal history is not, in itself, curative. Its purpose is to allow the patient and the analyst to discover the precise estrangement from self that those specific events seemed to require, and to learn what specific psychic mechanisms of defense the subject employed to accomplish that estrangement.

Armed with that cognitive awareness, supported by the analyst's trustable neutrality, now the work of undoing that defensive estrangement can proceed. Feelings and their specific attendant impulses toward action, cut off from awareness long ago, can now reemerge to be experienced by the subject once again. Feelings and impulses deemed too dangerous or forbidden at the age of two or four or ten, can be experienced and viewed in the light of a new and stronger day.

That is the process of cure in psychoanalytic treatment. Only by being open to the conscious experience of the full range of one's feelings can one hope to achieve the comfortable assurance that he can tolerate those feelings and manage himself appropriately and effectively under the pressure toward action that is part of those feelings. And then one need no longer be afraid of one's self.

OBSTACLES IN THE WAY

A great many people who could probably use psychoanalysis profitably never embark upon the course. Their reasons for that decision are varied, but they are often based upon mistaken notions about psychoanalysis and a lack of sufficient information about it.

The main source of resistance to the treatment stems from an underlying fear of novelty. Everyone who contemplates psychoanalytic treatment, even if it is only for the brief moment that it takes them to decide against it, gives it thought for one basic reason: that person wants his life to be better. But to want life to be better means that one must be willing to accept change. The wish for change is countered by the fear of novelty, and it is the balance between those two forces that largely determines the decision and the outcome of the analyses of those who decide to try as well.

Many are not aware of their fear of novelty and their resistance to psychoanalysis finds expression in other forms. The following discussion of a few of the more prevalent expressions of resistance is not meant primarily as an attempt to overcome those resistances but rather as an attempt to remove some of the mystery and the mistaken ideas that pervade the field.

Some, for example, claim to see psychoanalysis as a kind of self-indulgence by idle people who are too self-absorbed. Such a view reflects a moralistic judgment that emotional ills are not on a par with physical ills, for few who express this view would say the same about seeking the help of a physician for appendicitis or the crippling effect of a broken limb. They would accept that kind of self-indulgence, presumably because those ailments are physical and, therefore, beyond one's own control. Emotions, feelings, are assigned by them a lesser status: One is *supposed* to be strong enough to legislate one's own feelings. And many of those who espouse this view do continue to limp through life, pretending to be in control of their feelings. They control their feelings by keeping them locked away.

Another common expression of resistance takes the paradoxical position of reluctance to enter into the process because of concern about eventually having to give it up. Here the analyst is viewed as a "crutch" that they will never want to leave. I suspect there are very few who are reluctant to part with their real crutches when the need for them is gone. What is really involved here is the fear of feelings of dependency, the fear that those feelings are overwhelming and unresolvable. What looks like reluctance to enter into a close relationship with an analyst is but the specific expression of a far wider fear of allowing close relationships with anyone. Of course feelings of dependency are apt to arise, along with many other feelings, and they will all become a focus of analytic attention. Only through the process of familiarization can the goal of self-dependence be won.

Some are directly aware of their fear of the unknown. Will I discover things about myself that I'd rather not know? Will I become a worse person rather than a better one? Is it not better to let sleeping dogs lie?

Certainly one will discover things about one's self—that is the purpose of psychoanalysis. One must prefer knowledge to ignorance if one is to undertake the process. And analysis cannot make anyone worse—or better, in moralistic terms—

Psychoanalysis: Method and Goal

than one is. Analysis can only hope to familiarize you with who and what you already are. Then you can more effectively be yourself.

The concern about the cost of psychoanalysis—in terms of time, effort, and money—is sometimes legitimate and realistic. Yet this, too, is often a rationalization for many who spend far more on things that eventually afford much less happiness. One wishes that the treatment could be made more readily available to those who are really unable to afford it. There are a limited number of clinics that make analysis available at reduced fees and one hopes that trend will spread.

OBSTACLES ALONG THE WAY

There is also hope that removal of some of the mystery and the mistaken notions about psychoanalysis will facilitate and shorten the process, diminishing the cost by decreasing the trepidation of those who undertake the process. Some misinformation about psychoanalysis derives from inadvertence—the superficial or erroneous misreading of psychoanalytic literature. Some comes from the misguided efforts of the insufficiently informed who periodically attempt to popularize its concepts. And more misinformation is perpetrated by those who are antagonistic to its concepts—each for his individual reasons. But that is far from the whole story, for there is also a great deal of disagreement within the profession—among its own practitioners—about the means and ends of psychoanalysis. That disagreement within the profession adds greatly to the public's confusion.

The absence of a clear consensus about the curative factors in psychoanalysis creates an obscuring cloud. Some analysts believe the cure to be based upon the interpretation of resistance while others see the accurate reconstruction of past historical events to be the central issue. Some believe that the identification and proper interpretation of transference is the key to cure, and some believe that the empathy and relationship between analyst and analysand is what is important. I consider all of those elements to be important, but only as elements of technique, and no one of them or combination of them is able to explain the sought-after changes that take place in psychoanalytic treatment. That explanation lies implicit in the process of the analysis, a process that allows the resumption of self-familiarization interrupted long ago, and all of the elements mentioned above are important as they contribute to that process.

It is quite safe to say that all analysts are aware that feelings are important—extremely important—in analysis as in life. Yet, when discussions of the mechanisms of cure take place, feelings are rarely given center stage. Perhaps that is because there has not been a clear concept of what feelings are and how they operate within us. That ambiguity has led analysts, as well as the public, to consider feelings to be important and necessary *accompaniments* of other mental processes. Those other mental processes, being more available to observation, perhaps to measurement, seem more intellectually understandable, so they are made the central focus while feelings are assumed to somehow take care of themselves.

What is key to the process of cure is the conscious experience of feelings that were defensively cut off or muted long years before. And that is why a successful analysis cannot be conducted in a cool and intellectual manner. Some wish to approach it at arm's length, treating the process as though it were an exercise in problem solving similar to those in mathematics or in physics. But it is not sufficient simply to retrieve a coherent cognitive narrative of one's life history, nor is it enough to become even thoroughly aware of one's present foibles and behavioral eccentricities. That may enable the individual to know what actions to guard against, but it does not remove the need for the self-vigilance that defeats comfort and spontaneity.

Nor is analysis a matter of unrestrained emotional bloodletting. In the early days of psychiatry there was a period of time when emotional "catharsis" was popular. But catharsis failed, primarily because of its emphasis on "getting the feelings out," as though the feelings themselves were the pathogenic agents that had to be expunged. The feelings are not the problem. It is the fear of feelings, the effort to keep feelings from conscious awareness, that causes the problems.

Catharsis can afford some transient relief. The discharge of pent-up feelings—the expression of these feelings—does temporarily relieve tension, but it is the conscious experience of feelings that provides one with the opportunity to become familiar with those feelings. Then the individual can employ intellect, judgment, to determine appropriate and effective responses to the pressure of those feelings. Intellect and feeling are necessary partners in the analytic endeavor.

And so it is that analysts speak, among themselves, of the "therapeutic split in the Ego." That psychoanalytic jargon refers to the patient's ability to directly experience strong affect and, at the same time, to be intellectually and objectively aware of what is going on inside and out. Many have that capacity to some limited degree, but that skill grows as the analysis progresses.

Often the analyst is criticized, even jeered at, for his effort to remain always nonjudgmental, neutral, about conventional moral attitudes and values. It leads some, especially in movies and cartoons, to depict the analyst as inhuman, cold, removed. But there is very good reason for that stance of neutrality. It is meant to counter the existing cultural reinforcement of the tendency toward repression of feelings, an attitude that analysts have learned to overcome.

The repression of feelings is prompted not only by social opprobrium, but also by the individual's fear of the unpleasure that those feelings might create within himself. Whether one is motivated by fear of one's own unpleasure or by fear of the displeasure of the crowds, the repression of feelings results in the greater unpleasure of alienation from a central aspect of one's self. One has thereby crippled himself just as surely as he would do by amputating one of his limbs to avoid the possibility of pain from that part of himself. The primary goal of psychoanalytic treatment is the reparation of that self-amputation, not so that one might suffer the pain of that disaffected part of himself, but so that one might again become whole and learn to use that part of himself effectively.

Often it has been claimed that all varieties of therapy may have a positive effect, creating change and even cure. With that I have no argument, for there is no one circumstance that has exclusive power to initiate the resumption of development halted long before. Even the ordinary circumstances of life— an encounter with a good friend, a felicitous interaction with another person, a fortunate change in circumstances—may bring about the desired result. But they miss the point who try to use this as an argument against psychoanalysis. It does not deny the validity of that treatment. It only affirms that any circumstance that promotes the resumption of self-famil-iarization is effective, and I suggest that for many, psycho-analysis is best designed to accomplish that task most directly and effectively.

The work of psychoanalysis is the resumption of a learn-ing process that was interrupted at one or several points during childhood development. It is primarily a process of learning about one's own inner world of feelings, of becoming familiar with them, and of developing effective ways of han-dling them within the cultural context in which one lives.

THE OPENING PHASE

Each person who undertakes analysis brings to it a degree of trust in the analyst, a degree of trust variously determined

Psychoanalysis: Method and Goal

by his awareness of that analyst's salutory reputation, the respect he feels for the medical profession as a whole, or the confidence he feels in the certifying and licensing agencies involved, as well as the degree of trust that he feels toward people in general. And with that he brings his distrust of all those things as well, along with his distrust of the novel—for the analyst is, after all, a stranger.

The opening phase of the analysis, then, can reasonably be expected to be characterized predominantly by the testing that goes on. The patient has many questions. How does this stranger, the analyst, react? Will he be shocked by my revelations? Angered? Disgusted? Will he truly try to hear me and understand or will he be indifferent? Will he misuse me, humiliate me, hurt me, if I drop my guard? And so the patient begins the process of revealing himself, but with a sharp ear and eye for the analyst's actions and reactions.

For the analyst, this opening phase is a time for gathering information, largely from the patient's conscious verbalizations, but also from the myriad unconscious and nonverbal communications manifested in posture, tone, style, and patterns of association. The analyst's interventions are not so important now for the insights that they might avail but as evidence of the analyst's competence, serious intent, respect, and good will.

This is the phase of analysis in which there develops what has been called the "working alliance," essential for the subsequent massive work to be done. Except for the intensity and the self-awareness of the process in analysis, it is not unlike the process that always goes on in the developing close relationship between any two people.

This first phase of analysis is not time-limited nor is it sharply demarcated from the rest of the analysis. It is a continuous process of familiarization; the relationship is always, to some degree, on trial. But the necessity for testing diminishes with time as mutual trust develops and grows, and the major work of the analysis can now proceed.

THE MIDDLE PHASE

The ambience established by the analyst's trustable neutrality allows the patient greater freedom to turn his attention to inner matters. His greater familiarity with the external situation (the analyst and the analytic setting) allows him to deal with the risks of his internal situation more freely. He becomes less guarded against his repressed feelings and their attendant impulses which now approach conscious awareness, often signaling anxiety on the way.

The patient's discomfort is twofold. First of all, those feelings and impulses were originally repressed because they were deemed dangerous or unacceptable on their own account at that time, and their emergence now is greeted with anxiety, reflecting the fear that they originally engendered. A second and very important cause of discomfort now is the fear of inappropriateness, for those feelings and impulses repressed long ago have been cut off from conscious experience. So sequestered, they have not benefited from the maturational process which would allow for the development of more mature forms of expression.

Intense anger, for example, repressed at the age of three, seems as dangerously destructive now as it did then. Add to that the complicating fear that the anger will find expression in the form of a three-year-old's temper tantrum, and one senses the dilemma of the twenty- or forty-year-old patient who would feel shame about such inappropriate behavior.

We are dealing now with the main body of the analysis, the extensive middle phase in which most of the analytic work is accomplished. Freud once compared analysis with chess, saying that one could teach the opening moves and the endgame, but not the middle phase, for that was art.

Associations are verbalized, feelings arise and are recognized within a context, transference distortions become manifest, interpretations of resistance are made explicit, and reconstructions of the patient's history are formulated. As previously described, analysts' styles will vary and some will emphasize one or another of those elements over others, depending upon the particular analyst's conviction about which of those elements most effectively leads to change and cure.

The patient has an understandable reluctance to allow feelings free rein for he or she is now an adult, presumably capable of knowing appropriate behavior with others. The fear that the emergence of strong feelings might precipitate infantile or childish behavior that would be humiliating or dangerous reinforces the unconscious resistance to the emergence of those feelings. The unconscious resistance is primarily repression of those feelings and their associated ideas and impulses, but that is buttressed by a variety of character defenses that serve the maintenance of repression.

So one patient employs a character defense of intellectualization, viewing everything with a detached, clinical, and objective eye as though she and the analyst were together dispassionately viewing some specimen of mild interest. Another resorts to comedy and characteristically sees everything as a joke, hoping thereby to derail the process, while still another assumes his characteristic posture of helplessness and impotence, claiming to be unable to see or feel anything. And as strong feelings come closer to awareness, the intellectualizer becomes more coldly dispassionate, the comic more raucous, and the helpless more impotent.

These are characteristic behaviors that must be interpreted to the patient, for they have become so automatic that the patient is unaware of their defensive purpose and justifies them on rationalized grounds. Once the truth is known to both patient and analyst the defensive power of these behaviors is diminished, for little purpose is served by maintaining a pretense when both parties know its meaning.

Transference distortions begin to appear as strong feelings about the analyst begin to surface. Why, one might ask, do such strong feelings toward the analyst almost always arise?

Why are there so many jokes about the expectation that patients inevitably fall in love with their analysts? Let us start with the proposition that there is within everyone a very strong propensity to love, but that most are to some degree afraid of loving, and are frustrated by that fear of loving. Then those people encounter someone, the analyst, who is fair and caring, someone who clearly indicates his wish to help, someone who listens and really understands and who demonstrates at least a degree of wisdom. It is not difficult to understand that, under those circumstances, the defenses against loving begin to be weakened. Their innate tendency to love yields to the temptation of a situation that promises a degree of safety.

But it is only a degree of safety. Fear of loving continues to dictate caution. The analyst has been fair and caring and helpful, perhaps wise, up until now, but how will this person, whom I do not yet know thoroughly, react if I give in to my loving feelings? Fear still dictates caution, so the ancillary unconscious defense of transference distortion is called into play.

Rather than take the risk of loving in a novel situation, the patient quite unconsciously constructs, in the analyst's place, the image of a person that the patient does know quite thoroughly. Mother or father, sister or brother—it is someone whose reactions are very familiar to the patient. He knows what the limits are, and the expectations. If the need to defend against love is very strong, the patient may create the image of someone he hates, and then hate, anger, becomes a defense against loving. If the need to defend against love is less strong, then he may create the image of someone he does love, but in a controlled and limited way.

The complications of defense against feelings do not usually end there. Having constructed the image of a familiar figure in the analyst's place to defend against the feelings toward the analyst, the patient now finds himself confronting the image of someone who is familiar but toward whom he or she feels ambivalent, at least to some degree. Toward this unconsciously constructed image the patient finds himself experiencing old feelings of anger or jealousy, competitiveness, greed, or sexual desire. These feelings carry their own dangerous implications, even though they are directed toward a familiar image. So the patient now displaces the transference to some third party outside of the analytic situation. Distance makes the situation seem more safe.

So transference distortions tend to arise, at first, in displaced disguises. The patient complains that her boss, his wife, this or that friend or acquaintance, is too demanding, too intrusive, and allows him or her no free time or space. It is the analyst's task to recognize and interpret the displacement as a defense against the immediacy of those feelings in the analytic situation, to enable the patient to recognize that it is the analyst who he feels is invading his privacy.

Often the patient will resist that notion, insisting that his boss, her husband, the friend, really is too intrusive, too demanding, and that it is only the analyst's egocentricity that leads him to see everything to be focused upon him. The analyst must acknowledge that all of those reports about other people may well be so and that there is no intention of diminishing the importance of those external events, still, what is important to the ongoing process of the analysis is the recognition that the patient also is experiencing that feeling toward the analyst here and now.

As the defense of displacement of transference is overcome each time it occurs, the transference distortions are brought more directly into focus in the analytic setting, and the elaborations of those distortions enable the analyst to read the historical messages that they contain. This reenactment of the past in the present allows the analyst to reconstruct crucial events or circumstances in the patient's early relationships with significant figures, to understand the many interacting determinants that led the patient at specific times to repress specific feelings and their attendant impulses and thoughts.

The process of analysis here described is simplified to its bare bones, yet it describes the essential means by which repressions are uncovered, allowing the patient a broad perspective and understanding of how and why he came to be the way that he is. Yet the task is not complete, for there still remains the resolution of transference, and termination of the analysis short of that point will often avail the patient a fine intellectual grasp of his situation but little real change. I have the impression that analyses are often prematurely terminated at this level because of the failure to fully appreciate the central significance of the resolution of transference.

TERMINATION PHASE

The resolution of transference must not be considered a trivial loose end incidental to the process of psychoanalysis, for the substantial reduction of the need for transference is one of its fundamental goals. The continued existence of a propensity for transference distortion of the external world reflects the degree to which there is a continuing fear of being blind-sided by one's own feelings. And as long as that fear persists there will be a tendency to revert to repression of feelings once again when the safety and security of the analytic situation is gone. That person will have gained little comfort with himself and with his world.

When transference is incorrectly accepted as an expression of some mysterious repetition compulsion, postulated to be a basic biological principle, there can be no real resolution of transference. The most that can be hoped, then, is to instruct the patient about the particular transference distortions that he is apt to repeat, based upon his experience in the analysis. Andrea C., for example, would have to settle for an intellectual awareness of her propensity to misperceive others as though they were her father, mother, or younger sister, and then she would have to keep a watchful eye on herself to avoid repetition of those errors. Granted, that would be better than total lack of awareness of the tendency, but that result is less than one might desire. The wasteful effort of constant vigilance interferes with comfortable, easy spontaneity.

The recognition of transference as a defense against novelty allows the process to proceed to a deeper level. Now Andrea C. not only learns that she misperceives others in particular ways, but also discovers that she does so for a reason. She learns that she misperceives the present in terms of a familiar past so that she can avoid present feelings that she deems unsafe. As the analysis enables her to regain contact with those lost, repressed, feelings, to gain comfortable familiarity with them, her need to create an illusory familiarity disappears. Becoming comfortable with her inner world of feelings, she is free to acknowledge the significant novelties that she encounters in her present external world of events.

The specific and unique perceptual distortions of the individual are important for understanding his history. That one person sees his mother, another sees his grandmother, while a third sees his sister in each of the women that attract them, tells a specific historical tale. What is most important, however, is that none of them are then able to see these attractive women as the people that they are. The ultimate goal of analysis is the removal (or diminution) of the need for transference distortion in any form so that present objects may be perceived more clearly.

Inherent in this view of transference and its resolution there is an implicit suggestion of one significant dimension of psychological health: the capacity to accurately recognize the external world. Again, this accurate perception is not to be understood as a certainty of the essential nature of the universe in Platonic terms. Our construction of the external world is uniquely and peculiarly human, but it does work for us, allowing us to continue our adaptation to the world in which we live. Familiarity with our inner world of feelings and confidence in our ability to handle those feelings frees us to perceive the significant novelties of our external world.

Finally, what really does happen when it is time for patient and analyst to part? Is this truly a wrenching experience?

Must the patient mourn the loss of the much beloved analyst upon whom he or she became so intensely dependent? In short, the answer is no. At the end of the analysis they part as equals—they are two people who have come to know each other well and who care about each other.

Although aspects of the relationship between patient and analyst during the course of the analysis may bear a closer or more distant resemblance to the relationship between child and parent, all of that changes as the analysis works toward a close. The patient, having come to know and to trust himself, has gained the self-dependence, the self-confidence, that relieves him of excessive dependence upon others. Having been relieved of his fear of himself, he no longer believes that his survival rests upon the help he receives from others, including the analyst.

Relieved of his former fear of loving, he no longer has to see the analyst as the one and only safe object for his love. Now he is free to be interested in, to love, a wider world. That former love for the analyst is not totally dissipated but is placed in a broader perspective. It now assumes that form of love that we call friendship.

And gratitude is there, on both sides. The former patient is grateful to the analyst for his help in the effort to achieve this state of more effective function, of higher self-esteem. The analyst is grateful to his former patient for, having come to know this person so well, he has been taught something more about people than he could have known before.

Afterword: Happiness

The quest is for happiness, but the book primarily deals with issues that bear upon feeling good. The two, happiness and feeling good, are inextricably bound together in complicated ways, but there is a difference between them that must be made very explicit. Happiness is dependent upon the beneficence of the external world while feeling good is an internal matter, much more subject to individual control, and it is a prerequisite for happiness.

In the Introduction I spoke of health and wealth, fame and glory, hedonism, theology, political utopianism, all in relation to the quest for happiness. These are all externalities (taking the mind as our reference point) which I relegated to a position of secondary importance in the quest. It is not that they are unimportant, but simply that no one of them and no combination of them will, by itself, bring happiness. Feeling good must be there first, and then fortunate external circumstances will fulfill the goal.

On the other hand, feeling good is not itself sufficient for happiness, for no matter how good one may feel about one's self, the existence of sufficient adversity prevents one from being happy. Political, social or economic oppression, the loss of loved ones, natural catastrophes, do preclude happiness for even those who may feel very good about themselves.

One may argue, however, that fortunate circumstance and

206

Afterword: Happiness

feeling good have an interacting effect; that fame and glory, for example, can make one feel good. Yes it can, but that is only a very fleeting effect, for the applause of the crowds is soon gone and then one must search for ever more applause, and that is often an exhausting and a most frustrating pursuit. Wasn't Marilyn Monroe a living, and dying, example of that? And wealth, alone, certainly doesn't fill the bill. It is much more likely that the person who feels good about himself will be able to create the fortunate external circumstances that bring happiness than the other way around, but even this has its ultimate limitation. Some of those who were victims of Hitler's Germany, for example, may have felt good about themselves but they certainly were not happy in the death camps. Still, we must recognize that most of those who escaped in time probably were able to do so because they felt good enough to try.

In this quest for happiness, many will find it difficult to shift their conscious gaze to the inner world of the mind for we are much more accustomed to search consciously for things outside. Perhaps that is a consequence of evolution and of history, man's early survival having depended primarily on his ability to perceive our outside world clearly. Yet, we are not without the tools for looking inside. Indeed, we are and always have been very sensitively attuned to our inner processes, for how else can we understand that man always has been moved by his own inner feelings? To be moved by his feelings he always must have been aware of them. The problem is that he has not always been *consciously* aware of them, and when he has been conscious of them he often did not realize that those feelings were his own. Indeed, in ancient times man believed that the feelings that moved him were created by external forces, sometimes demonic, sometimes divine, and many today continue that belief. That is not a result of some simple stubborn clinging to superstition and myth, but rather an expression of man's universal wish to understand cause and effect in the service of mastery. Not understanding the personal and internal origin of his feelings, he sought, and still often seeks, an explanation in the external world.

However, it would be naive for us to believe that custom born of history is, alone, responsible for man's persistent external focus. One often meets strong resistance from those who are reminded that their feelings are their own and who are directly encouraged to look inside. Often, people do not want to know what's there; either they fear their feelings or, under the influence of culture's misdirected civilizing intent, they prejudge their feelings to be evil or shameful. And so custom becomes reinforced by the wish to not know.

Psychoanalysis courageously broke some of the conventional strictures that block our full view of humankind and we are deeply in its debt for the broad insights that it thus revealed. Yet candor demands that we acknowledge how far psychoanalysis, too, has yet to go. Errors remain embedded in its theory, errors that stem largely from its inability to always stand at a sufficient critical distance from conventional morality and bias. Although it strives always to be nonjudgmental, conventional negative views of man keep creeping into its fabric. Aggression, often meaning hostility and destructiveness, is put on a par with love, the two being assigned equal status as fundamental drives in the motivation of man. Love and sexuality have remained conventionally locked, and man's egocentricity is not recognized as a secondary and compensatory defensive mechanism but is viewed as something intrinsic. Narcissism (excessive self-love) is elevated from psychopathology to a component of normal development. The id is viewed with veiled suspicion as a caldron of infantile yearnings that have to be curbed by society's "civilizing" intent. The adult is seen as an infant grown large and covered over with a thin costume of culture, waiting always for an opportunity to regress to some imagined early blissful state. And the infant continues to be misperceived as an egomaniacal imperious tyrant who has yet to be whipped into shape to be considered fully human.

The acceptance of the fact that man is from the start a

loving and generous creature will do much to relieve his prevalent fear of his feelings. Then the infant will be treated with respect, as well as with love, and he will be trusted to continue to be human as he grows and develops. In that atmosphere he will continue to experience the full range of his feelings as maturation and experience allow him to learn increasingly effective and acceptable forms for their expression in behavior. Most importantly, he will not be forced to fear his own feelings. Then the energy and vitality of feelingfulness will be his, and so will the conviction that he is, and can be, his own person. He will achieve a high level of autonomy, self-mastery, which will earn his high self-esteem, and he will be free to be intensely interested, to love. Being unafraid of himself he will therefore have little fear of novelty and will be able to perceive his world clearly and objectively, and that will allow him to make his own breaks in the real world most effectively. His will be the best hope for happiness.

For those already grown up, the way is more complicated. Most have already suffered too much the indignity of helplessness, the shame of being humiliated and trivialized, the frustration of unaccepted natural longings, the disappointment of love rejected, and have sought to protect themselves from repeated hurt and heartbreak by building walls, inside and out. In so doing they have achieved only alienation; alienation from a vital part of themselves and, secondarily, from their fellow men. The limited space they allow themselves within their self-constructed walls is chronic boredom, and that is a very lonely space. When one cannot even have access to himself, that is the ultimate loneliness.

But even the alienated and chronically bored need not despair. Just as their feelings belong to them, so do their self-constructed walls. Once erected, those repressing walls tend to be stubbornly persistent, but they are not impenetrable. It requires a persistent attempt to see through them, to look at what lies behind them, to knock those walls down, but that can be and has been done. It often requires outside help as well; the help of spouse or friend or mentor or psychoanalyst whose respectful acceptance of the individuals' feelings will facilitate their own acceptance of their feelings, enabling them to turn their attention to where they feared to look before. And as the walls of repression begin to crumble, those people will experience the return of feelingfulness, of liveliness, that allows the resumption of the search for happiness.

Happiness is a real and achievable goal for man but the first step is the requirement that the human change his conventional view of human nature. That will not be an easy task, but it is not an impossible one. The human, being human, already knows the truth about what it is to be human. He has only to be reminded of what he already knows but does not yet know that he knows; to be reminded of the truth that the conventions of culture and of history have distorted and clouded over.

References

Abraham, K. (1921), Contribution to the theory of the anal character. *Selected Papers on Psychoanalysis*. London: Hogarth Press, 1949.

——— (1924), Influence of oral erotism on character formation. *Selected Papers on Psychoanalysis*. London: Hogarth Press, 1949.

Alexander, F. (1948), *Fundamentals of Psychoanalysis*. New York: W.W. Norton and Co., 1948.

Benedek, T. (1967), on the psychic economy of developmental processes. *AMA Archives of General Psychiatry*, 17(3):271–276.

Bernstein, H. (1975), Boredom and the ready-made life. *Social Research*, Autumn 1975, vol. 42, no. 3, pp. 512–537.

Camus, A. (1956), *The Fall*. New York: Random House, 1956, p. 37.

Crews, F. (1972), Offing culture: Literary study and the movement. *Northwestern University Tri-Quarterly:* No. 23 & 24, p. 36.

Dostoyevsky, F. (1864), *Notes from Underground*. New York: Dell Publishing Co., 1960, p. 45.

Erikson, E. (1950), *Childhood and Society*. New York: W.W. Norton & Co., 1950, p. 219.

Fenichel, O. (1934), Zur Psychologie der Langeweile. *Imago* 20:270–281.

Ferenczi, S. (1913), *Stages in the Development of the Sense of Reality: Selected Papers of Sandor Ferenczi*. New York: Basic Books, 1950, Vol. 1: 213–239, p. 216.

French, T. (1952), *Integration of Behavior*. Chicago: University of Chicago Press, 1952, vol. 1, p. 51.

Freud, S., & Breuer, J. (1893), Studies in Hysteria. Standard Edition. London: Hogarth Press, 1955, 3: 250–251.

References

Freud, S., and Breuer, J., (1893), On the Psychichal Mechanisms of Hysterical Phenomenon. Standard Edition. London: Hogarth Press, 1955, 2:7

Freud, S., (1901), Psychopathology of everyday life. *Standard Edition*, 6. London: Hogarth Press, 1960.

—— (1908a), "Civilized" sexual morality and modern nervousness. *Standard Edition*, 9:188. London: Hogarth Press, 1959.

—— (1908b), Character and anal erotism. *Standard Edition*, 9:169. London: Hogarth Press, 1959.

—— (1912), Dynamics of transference. *Standard Edition*, 12:99–108. London: Hogarth Press, 1958.

—— (1914), On narcissism, An introduction. *Standard Edition*, 14:69. London: Hogarth Press, 1957.

—— (1915a), The unconscious. *Standard Edition*, 14:179f. London: Hogarth Press, 1957.

—— (1915b), Repression. *Standard Edition*, 14:143–158. London: Hogarth Press, 1957.

—— (1915c), Instincts and their vicissitudes. *Standard Edition*, 14:123. London: Hogarth Press, 1957.

—— (1916), Some character types met with in psychoanalytic work. *Standard Edition*, 14:311. London: Hogarth Press, 1957.

—— (1920), Beyond the pleasure principle. *Standard Edition*, 18:12. London: Hogarth Press, 1955.

—— (1926), Inhibition, symptom and anxiety. *Standard Edition*, 20:83. London: Hogarth Press, 1959.

—— (1930), Civilization and its discontents. *Standard Edition*, 21:59. London: Hogarth Press, 1961.

—— (1933), New introductory lectures. *Standard Edition*, 22:80. London: Hogarth Press, 1964.

Greenacre, P. (1960), Considerations regarding the parent-infant relationship, *International Journal of Psychoanalysis*, 41:571–584.

Greenson, R. (1963), On boredom, *Journal of the American Psychoanalytic Association*, 1:7–21.

Groddek, G. (1923), The Book of the It. New York: Mentor Books, 1961, p. 19.

Jung, C. G. (1916), *Psychology of the Unconscious*. New York: Moffat, Yard, 1916. Introduction, B. M. Hinkle, pp. 27–28. Also: Part 2, Chapter 2, p. 139.

—— (1936), *Modern Man in Search of a Soul*. London: Kegan, Paul, 1936, p. 138.

Kohut, H. (1971), *Analysis of the Self.* New York: International Universities Press, 1971.

Mahler, M. (1965), Mother-child interaction during separation-individuation. *Selected Papers of Margaret S. Mahler.* New York: Jason Aronson, 1979, p. 45.

Nietzsche, F. (1888), The antichrist. *The Complete Works of Friedrich Nietzsche,* editor Oscar Levy. New York: Russel and Russel, 1964, 16:197.

Pope, A. (1733–34), An essay on man. *Standard Edition,* edited by W. Elwin and W. Courthope, London: J. Murray, 1871–1889. Epistle 4: line 255.

Reich, W. (1928), On character analysis. *The Psychoanalytic Reader,* editor, R. Fliess. New York: International Universities Press, 1948, pp. 129–181.

Reich, W. (1929), The Genital Character and the Neurotic Character. New York: University Press, 1948. pp. 148–169.

———— (1930), Character formation and phobias of childhood. *The Psychoanalytic Reader,* editor, R. Fliess. New York: International Universities Press, 1948, p. 179.

Thoreau, H. D. (1854), *Walden,* Boston & New York: Houghton Mifflin Co., 1900. Vol 2. p. 15.

Twain, M. (1906), *What Is Man?* New York: DeVinne, 1906. Chapter 6.

Index

Abraham, K., 12
Adaptation
  and feelings, 35
Adolescence
  and boredom, 91
  and judgment, 185
  and pre-adolescent, 185
Adult Development, 186
Affectivity, 34
Aggression, 108, 130, 207
Alexander, F., 127, 128, 163
Alienation
  and chronic boredom, 63
Anaclitic Love, 146
Analysis, 103
Anger, 108
Anxiety
  and fear, 59
  cycles of, 100
  defined, 55
  regulation of tension, 49
  significance of, 54
Apathy
  and chronic boredom, 63,
    110
Assertiveness, 130
Autonomous Man, 148
Autonomy
  and conscious awareness, 146
  and creativity, 146
  and happiness, 143
  defined, 4
Avoidance
  the illusion of, 111
  regulation of, 50

Benedek, T., 164
Bernard, C., 42
Bernstein, H., 174
Boredom

chronic, 6, 53, 58, 60
  cycles of, 100
  depression of, 108
  defined, 54
  regulation of tension, 49
  as signal feeling, 42
Brillance, 170

Camus, A., 65
Cannon, W., 42
Catharsis, 194
Character
  and chronic boredom, 92
  defenses, 93
  neurosis, 93, 94
  structure, 94
  study of, 15
Child Development
  and chronic boredom, 74
  and communication, 159
  and helplessness, 161
  and "optimal frustration",
    162
  and the maligned infant, 154
  and mastery, 159
  and trust, 161
  and permissiveness, 169
  and tact, 169
Choice
  freedom of, 144
Chronic boredom, 6, 53, 58
  and adolescence, 92
  and alienation, 63
  and apathy, 63
  and child development, 74,
    180
  and character, 92, 95
  a concept of, 78
  and confrontation, 71
  depression of, 96, 138

(unpleasure) as signal feeling, 42, 45
Perception, 114, 122
Permissiveness, 169
Physiological disequilibrium, 43
Platonic Idealism, 115
Pleasure
  and pain, 45
  "principle", 45, 147
Pope, A., 19
Possession
  and love, 139
  and the child, 168
Psychic discharge, mechanism of regulation, 50
Psychic tension, 52, 94
Psychoanalysis, 77, 147, 157, 166, 182, 189, 207
Psychology
  Adlerian, 145
  psychoanalytic, 13, 14
  theory, 14, 143

"Reality Principle", 147
Regulation
  avoidance, 50
  mechanisms of, 50
  psychic discharge, 50
Reich, W., 12, 92, 94, 149
Rejection, fear of, 133
Relationships, interpersonal, 4
Repetition compulsion, 7
Repression, 5, 41, 52, 56, 95, 107, 111, 201
Resistance, 199
Rorschack ink blots, 115

Self-discipline
  and child development, 177

learning, 177
  as a positive value, 177
Self-esteem, 3, 17
  basis of, 23
  child's, 183, 185
  high, 24, 136, 150, 175, 208
  loss of, 137
  low, 24, 141, 175, 185
  others', 18
  reinforcement of, 135
Self-evaluation
  the "double", 22
Self-familiarization, 189
Self-judgement, 3, 19
Self-mastery, 4, 26, 48, 145, 177
Self-organization, 25
Self-psychology, 156
Sensations
  and boredom, 104
  in infancy, 164
  versus feelings, 31
Separateness
  in toddlers, 167
Sex, and chronic boredom, 65
Sexual desire
  and excitement, 55
  and feelings, 47
Signal feelings, 41
  as boredom, 41
  as excitement, 41
  as pain, 41
  as pleasure, 41
Social disequilibrium, 35, 43
Social roles
  and adolescence, 186
Stimulus hunger, 63
Super ego, and choice, 147
Surplus energy, 128, 163
Surprise, the element of, 121
Suppression, 53, 60